CRACKING
THE
BOOK

CRACKING
THE
BOOK
HOW TO START READING THE BIBLE

J. MARK LAWSON

TRUSTED
BOOKS
A DIVISION OF DEEP RIVER BOOKS

Trusted Books is an imprint of Deep River Books. The views expressed or implied in this work are those of the author. To learn more about Deep River Books, go online to www.DeepRiverBooks. com.

All scripture quotations, unless otherwise noted, are taken from *New Revised Standard Version Bible*, ©1989 by the Division of Christian Education of the National Council of the Churches of Christ in the United States of America.

ISBN 13: 978-1-63269-084-5
Library of Congress Catalog Card Number: 2010912941

The author wishes to thank Larry Isbell, Marjorie Purnine, Jim Krisher, Richard Scheffler, and Paul Herpich for their encouragement, support, and valuable input into this project.

CONTENTS

FOREWORD

MANY SCHOLARS, MINISTERS, and other church leaders from across the theological spectrum have written introductions to the Scriptures, but few have written introductions to *reading* the Scriptures. The best of Christian writers have made worthy efforts to give beginning readers a compass for getting around the Bible. But as far as I can tell, few have succeeded in offering an introduction to reading the Bible that is brief, plain, and clear—yet intellectually responsible. This is probably because the people who are qualified to write such an introduction have lived with the Scriptures for so long that they have forgotten how intimidating the Bible is to those who have never or rarely read it.

In the nearly quarter century I have served as a pastor, I have found that my preaching and teaching ministry largely concerns biblical literacy training. As our culture becomes increasingly post-Christian, the basic biblical narrative is no longer common knowledge. First-time visitors to church are as likely to be familiar with the Old and New Testaments as with the ancient writings of Thucydides. Even people who attend church every week, and who hear the Scriptures read publicly, may be no more capable of finding the gospel of Luke in the Bible than locating specific regulations in the federal tax code.

Biblical literacy is not a measure of a person's morality or faith commitment. It is, however, important in building communities of faith. The Bible is a book about God's relationship to people. Over and over, the Scriptures make clear that God relates to each of us by relating to all of us. Both the Old and New Testaments teach that love of God and love of one another are inextricably bound—like two sides of the same coin. To enter the world of the Bible is to join a communion of saints that stretches back many centuries, and to learn from them what it means to live in covenant with God. Our quality of life in present-day faith communities is greatly enhanced when we share a bond with the people of God in the Scriptures.

As I prepare weekly sermons, I realize I will be addressing people with a wide diversity of knowledge of the biblical text. Some have been nurtured with a steady diet of biblical preaching and Bible study. Others have *heard* enough to follow references to biblical characters and stories—but have little facility with the text itself. Still others will experience the day's Scripture texts as fresh literature. Often people from the latter two groups tell me how utterly ill-equipped they feel to join a Bible study group, let alone open the Bible and start reading it on their own. It is my task as a preacher to speak to and challenge all who gather for worship, regardless of how much or little of the Bible they know. As a teacher, I have the further responsibility to encourage biblical literacy. In some cases, this means helping people overcome intimidation and start reading the Bible for the first time.

My purpose in this short book is not to give a full introduction to the Bible or to Bible study. My purpose is only to give a brief overview of Scripture for those who have never read it—or whose only exposure has been hearing it or following along as it is read in worship. I have purposely left many questions unanswered and many issues unresolved. I have resisted every temptation to delve more deeply than a first-time Bible reader is ready to go. The text is, by design, completely free of footnotes.

I have tried to reflect responsible scholarship. My desire was to write briefly and simply enough not to intimidate, yet broadly enough to encourage further study. Perhaps this primer will help to reduce just a bit the rate of biblical illiteracy. Above all, I hope that it will encourage more conversation with and about God by making the Scriptures a little more accessible.

—J. Mark Lawson

CHAPTER 1

GETTING STARTED

W HEN YOU PICK up a Bible, what are you holding?

Somewhere on the cover, almost always on the spine, you will find the title "Holy Bible." Both words are important. "Bible" comes from the Greek word *biblia*, which means "books." The Bible, therefore, is not one book. It is a collection of many books. These books are "holy," meaning they are sacred writings. Christians have historically referred to these writings as "the Word of God." Though this phrase means different things to different groups, there is broad consensus in Christianity that the inspiration for the words that make up these writings comes from God. Some of the Bible's books were written over a long period by many authors. Others were written by only one person in a short period. Regardless of the process by which they came into being, every book in the Bible is there, Christians believe, because God was somehow involved in the process.

Of course, non-Biblical writings might also be judged as inspired by God. The world's great poetry and fiction often lift their readers to spiritual heights and, through the talent of the authors, bear witness to the presence of the divine. What is different about the books of the Bible is that they serve the specific purpose of calling their readers into relationship with God. So, not only are they written under divine inspiration, but they also summon people toward God. Different books in the Bible serve this purpose in different ways, but the entire Bible has as its main purpose to prompt, nurture, and deepen a relationship between the readers and God. So in a very real sense, the Bible is one way that God speaks to us. This is why the Bible is referred to as "the Word of God."

Another name for the Bible is "the Scriptures," which means "the writings." When the word *scripture* is capitalized, it refers to sacred writings, such as the Bible.

Translations of the Bible

Also on the spine, or on one of the opening pages, you will find the name of a translation, such as "King James Version," "New Revised Standard Version," or "New International Version." Today there are dozens of such translations. The Bible was first written in Hebrew, Aramaic, and Greek. Until the invention of the printing press, most people did not read the Bible because they were illiterate. There was no incentive for most people to learn how to read, because the parchment on which books were hand-written was very expensive. Reading was only for the wealthy and for scholars. Before the sixteenth century, the Bible had been translated out of its original languages only once. In the fourth century, one of the church's leading scholars, Jerome, translated the Bible into Latin—the common language of the Roman Empire in which he lived. This translation was called the "Vulgate," because it was written in the common ("vulgar") language of the people.

The Vulgate became the church's official translation, so that even after Latin ceased to be a live language, the Bible was read only by scholars and only in Latin. It is ironic that the translation into a common tongue became accessible only to the educated elite. But as long as books remained an expensive luxury, there was no widespread interest in translating the Bible into any other language.

Gutenberg's printing press, however, made books affordable. People quickly began learning how to read. One of reformer Martin Luther's first publications was the Bible, translated into his native tongue of German. It was only a matter of time before translations of the Bible in all the languages of Europe were being mass-produced. Some of these translations were taken from the Vulgate. Others made use of old Hebrew, Greek, and Aramaic documents like the ones Jerome had used. These were not the original texts, but copies dating back to the fourth century.

The most famous such translation from early texts is the one authorized by King James of England in 1603 and completed in 1611. For this masterpiece of English literature, the king assembled an impressive panel of scholars. The King James Version would become the most beloved Bible translation for English-speaking people, and even today, when its Elizabethan English is difficult to read, continues to be the translation of choice for many British and American Christians.

Most other English translations date from the end of the nineteenth century or more recently. Over the past two centuries, the field of archeology has uncovered earlier documents than were available to the King James translators. We will probably never find any of the Bible's original manuscripts, but in many cases, archeologists have come close. Scholars now have access to manuscripts that date to within 100 years of the life of Christ. They also work with multiple documents that date to roughly the same time, so they are able to compare copies and ascertain with increasing accuracy what the original manuscripts said.

Because archeology continues to uncover new evidence about the Bible, new translations are continually undertaken. In addition, new translations are required by changes in modern English. As the meanings of words change and new idioms emerge, people need updated translations so the Bible remains readable and understandable.

Many people are troubled by so many translations because it is difficult to judge which are the most reliable. Keep in mind that better than 98 percent of these translations are the same in meaning, if not in wording. It is amazing that the Bible has not undergone any more changes than it has in two thousand years. The differences in translation need not concern novice readers of Scripture. These are issues for advanced Bible study, and they have little bearing on the Bible's central themes.

Getting Around the Bible

When you thumb through the Bible, you will find the names of the various books at the tops of pages. You will also find a series of numbers. These refer to chapter and verse divisions within the Bible. While not part of the original manuscripts, these divisions serve as helpful reference points for finding particular sections. Medieval scribes added them to make the Bible easier to study.

As we have it today, we can view the Bible as one whole with many different levels. First, the Bible is divided into two major sections: the Old Testament and the New Testament (also called "the Hebrew Scriptures" and "the Christian Scriptures"). In non-Catholic versions, the Old Testament contains the same writings as the Jewish Bible, though in a slightly different order. These 39 books make up about three-quarters of the Bible.

The Catholic version of the Old Testament includes an additional 15 books that were written in Greek rather than Hebrew—and were not accepted as Scripture by early Jewish scholars. These fifteen books, usually referred to as the "Apocrypha" (the name Jerome gave them when he translated the Bible into Latin), are considered of a different nature than the other books. I will introduce those books that are common to all Christian editions of the Old Testament, and include a separate section that explains the Apocrypha.

The New Testament consists of 27 books that deal exclusively with the beginnings of Christianity—from the time of Jesus through the first century of the church's development.

Except for some very short ones, each book of the Bible is divided into chapters. These are not nearly as long as most chapters in contemporary books. Often, but not always, they divide material into logical sections. Their primary purpose is to aid the reader in locating passages. Each chapter is further divided into verses. Verses are often only one sentence, and seldom more than two. Some verses contain only part of a sentence.

Verses allow people who are writing about or quoting Scripture to be precise in their citations. For instance, when I quote the "golden rule" (Do unto others as you would have them do unto you), I might tell you it is found in the Bible. But if you wanted to find it yourself, that would not be very helpful. Even if I told you it is found in the New Testament book of Matthew, you still would be hard-pressed to locate it. But if I tell you it is found in Matthew 7:12 (chapter 7, verse 12), you can locate it exactly. You can also read it in its larger context and gain a deeper meaning of this saying. Depending on what translation you have, you are likely to find it does not read precisely as it is usually quoted in popular culture.

Where Do I Begin?

If you are reading the Bible for the first time, you might assume that you should start where you would with any other book—at the beginning. First-time readers who choose this approach often give up before they've gotten through Leviticus (the third book) because the task of reading the Bible cover-to-cover can be arduous (and often boring), especially if you don't really know what you're reading about.

The Bible's most accessible entry point is not at the beginning, but in the middle. Popular editions of the Bible often include lots of "study notes" at the bottom of the pages, changing the amount of material between the covers. If you have a Bible that includes only the actual text, and you open it to the middle, you will be in the Psalms. "Psalms" comes from the Greek word meaning "songs."

The book of Psalms is the hymnbook of the people of the Old Testament and the New Testament. We no longer have the original musical notations, but the lyrics invite us into the world of the Scriptures with their beautiful poetry. They are not only songs; they are also prayers that express a wide range of emotions to God.

After you have gained a sense of the Old Testament, you will read the psalms differently. You will find within them references to the history of Israel, and you might be able to relate specific psalms to certain events in the Old Testament. But there is value in approaching the psalms without any context. Like all great poetry, the psalms speak powerfully to the human condition—both in times of joy and in times of despair.

If the purpose of the Scriptures is to invite us into a relationship with God, then the psalms are like greeters standing at the door of the Bible with hands outstretched, waiting to escort us into God's presence. We need no preparation. The psalms speak to God for us. They tell God of our hopes, our dreams, our pain, our fear, our shame, and our gratitude. They express the full range of human emotion. Some of the psalms make us uncomfortable because they express feelings that seem unacceptable for people of faith.

They teach us there is no feeling we cannot express to God; that prayer and worship should involve our whole selves, not just that part we feel good about. Through the psalms, we learn to bring to God even those parts of ourselves we are ashamed of or confused about. Only then can we expect God to transform us completely.

In the Bible's numbering system, each psalm is treated as a chapter and numbered separately. So rich are these prayers that you could start anywhere. You could let the pages of your Bible fall open to any psalm and just begin reading until you find one that seems to resonate with your spirit. But if you prefer a little more direction, begin with those numbered 23 (the most famous), 27, 30, 51, 77, 100, 121, and 148.

Spend time with the psalms, especially those that express your own thoughts and feelings. Read them several times silently, and if you are alone, read them out loud. Let these ancient words of God's people begin your conversation with God.

Getting the Whole Story

Once you have been ushered into the Scriptures, and you understand the numerical reference system of chapters and verses, you will want to try to gain an understanding of the Bible's overall contents. When you turn to the table of contents, you will see a long list of books. (Some editions have separate tables of contents for each testament.) But you need more than the names of the books to know where to continue reading. The next two chapters will summarize the contents of the Old and New Testaments.

For each section, I provide a list of "essential" readings. By "essential," I mean those portions of Scripture that will give you a basic understanding of the Christian faith. As I said, if you try to read the entire Bible cover to cover, you are likely to get discouraged. But if you read the texts I list, you will get a good sense of the overarching narrative of the Scriptures, and how the ministry of Jesus and early Christian teachings fit into that story. (In no way do I mean to suggest that other texts are unimportant. In fact, reading these essential texts will likely whet your appetite.)

The edge of the Judean wilderness overlooking the Dead Sea.
The patriarchs traveled in this wilderness, and just to
the north the Israelites crossed the Jordan
River to settle the Promised Land.

CHAPTER 2

THE OLD TESTAMENT

THE OLD TESTAMENT, sometimes referred to as the "Hebrew Scriptures," was written over a period of about 1000 years. The oldest writings began as stories that were passed down orally from generation to generation. Though the stories date back to about 1800 years before Christ, most scholars believe they were not written down until about 1000 years before Christ, and even then, the accounts were not in the form we now have in the Bible.

A large portion of the Old Testament, extending from the book of Genesis through the book of 2 Kings, represents a careful piecing together of several written sources that had developed over a long period. Different tribes within the nation of Israel had preserved their own versions of the stories about how Israel became a kingdom. The scribes who compiled the books of the Old Testament wove these versions together, recognizing that more than one perspective on these events was truthful. The presence of multiple versions of the same events sometimes confuses readers, because it seems the Bible is contradicting itself.

We find an example of this in 1 Samuel. In chapter 8, God is clearly opposed to Israel having a king and tells Samuel (Israel's judge and priest) to discourage it. But chapter 9 shows God in favor of a king, even choosing who will be crowned. An early scribe has included two versions of the story. One tradition held that God never wanted a king. The other believed that the kingship was God's plan. When both traditions are included, a third perspective emerges: God was opposed to a king, but when the people persisted in demanding one, God chose a king for them, since it was clear they were going to have one with or without God's permission.

The biblical story, therefore, contains an important lesson that readers could not have gleaned from either tradition by itself. God guides us to make the right choices, but even when we insist on making wrong ones, God does not abandon us. God is with us even when we suffer the consequences of our poor choices. In the midst of our trials, God continues to guide us, leading us back to the right path.

The Old Testament is full of examples like this, where two traditions of very different perspectives are woven together to yield a deeper meaning to the events. This process of weaving together traditions, what scholars call "redaction," is as much inspired by God as the writings themselves.

The first five books of the Old Testament (Genesis, Exodus, Leviticus, Numbers, and Deuteronomy) make up the first major section of the Bible. For many years, these five books, called "the Torah" in Hebrew, made up the entire Jewish Bible. "Torah" means "law." The central concern of these books is to spell out the laws by which God intends people to live. Therefore, the focal point of the Torah is the Ten Commandments, found in Exodus 20:1-17 (and repeated in Deuteronomy 5:6-21). These are the ten basic rules necessary for being in relationship to God.

The Ten Commandments are immediately followed in chapters 21-23 of Exodus by a long list of other commandments, including many that seem strange and irrelevant to contemporary readers. The book of Leviticus is made up entirely of such regulations, as are large portions of Numbers and Deuteronomy. Altogether, the five books of the Torah contain 613 separate commandments, but the Torah consists of more than laws for the nation Israel. It also contains stories that lie at the heart of our faith.

Beginnings

Essential Readings: Genesis 1:1-5:2; 6:5-9:19; 11:1-9

The first eleven chapters of Genesis concern the beginnings of history. Here we find the stories of creation, Adam and Eve, Cain and Abel, and Noah's Ark. This opening section of the Bible is one of the most controversial. Debates have raged over whether we should interpret the creation account literally or as a story, much like Greek myths, which are not historical but do communicate important truth. Within both Catholicism and Protestantism, Christians have taken one of three basic positions.

Many conservative Christians insist that unless Genesis 1 is historically true, it cannot be true at all. They resist any suggestion that there are different kinds of truth or different ways of communicating it. To hold this position, one must reject evolution as an explanation of how life came into being. Those who hold to a literal view of Genesis 1 therefore refer to themselves as "Creationists."

Many liberal Christians take the position that Genesis 1 is simply a poetic expression of the nature of the human experience and its moral dilemmas. In this view, none of the stories in the first eleven chapters of Genesis has any relationship to history; they are simply parables about life.

A third approach many Christians take is to recognize that the creation account is not intended as history, but it does display more than just a figurative truth. For instance, the six "days" of creation do not necessarily refer to solar days, since the sun is not created until the third day. So they might refer to great eons of natural development. (The order in which life forms emerge in Genesis 1 is strikingly parallel to the order described by evolutionary biology: first sea creatures, then four-legged land creatures, then upright human beings.)

Even if we can make some connection between science and Genesis 1, it is important to remember that the purpose of Genesis 1, as part of the Bible, is to bring us into relationship with God. Its purpose is not scientific, but theological. So regardless of how you interpret Genesis 1, you will not receive its message unless you ask what it says about the relationship between God and the world. The text is really about that relationship.

ADAM AND EVE IN THE GARDEN OF EDEN

Scholars have long noted that Genesis contains two creation stories. The first one (first in the text but probably composed later) extends through chapter 2, verse 3. Then another version of creation begins in 2:4. There are striking differences between these two. In the first, the human race is created last and is celebrated as God's crowning achievement, made in God's image. In the second, human beings are made before there were plants or animals, and they are formed "from the dust of the ground" (2:7). So while the first creation story emphasizes how humanity is created "from above," the second describes man and woman created "from below." Placed side by side, these two stories witness our dual nature: transcendent yet limited, both spirit and body.

Another important difference between the two stories concerns the use of the Hebrew word *adam*. In Genesis 1, *adam* means "humankind" (1:26). The word refers to the entire human race. In the second story, *adam* is a proper name and refers to a specific person. "Adam" and his mate "Eve" are pictured as the father and mother of the human race, from which all of us descend. Their story, therefore, is our story. Creationists take Adam and Eve to be literal people, so that the human race did not evolve but was created all at once. Others view Adam and Eve as archetypal figures of humanity.

Whether you see Adam and Eve as historical figures or figurative representations of humanity, the truth of their story is the same. They enjoy an idyllic relationship with one another, the created order, and God. Then they violate the limits God set for them and suffer grave consequences. Adam and Eve are filled with shame, alienated from God, and expelled from the garden where God had placed them. From the moment of their first act of disobedience, all their relationships—with God, with creation, and with one another—become skewed. Further, their act of disobedience cannot be contained. Their "sin" (alienation from God) spreads to their progeny. In chapter 4, one of their sons, Cain, murders another son, Abel, out of jealousy. After the story of the first human family, chapter 5 lists the descendants of Adam down to the time of Noah. This genealogy serves the purpose of illustrating that as the human race multiplied, so did humanity's sinful behavior.

GOD'S COVENANT WITH NOAH

Much of the opening section of the Bible concerns the story of a great flood whose only survivors were Noah, his family, and all the animals he gathered onto an ark built to exact specifications he received from God. "Noah's ark" has inspired many children's books and is familiar to many people who have never read the Bible. This story, however, is really not so much about Noah or his famous ark and all the animals it housed. Like the rest of Scripture, it is about our relationship to God.

God sends the flood because "the wickedness of human-kind was great in the earth, and ... every inclination of the thoughts of their hearts was only evil continually." Because of this hopeless situation, "The Lord was sorry that he had made humankind on the earth, and it grieved him to his heart" (Genesis 6:5-6). So God chooses the only "righteous man" left, Noah, to build an ark big enough for Noah's family and two of every species of animal. God the Creator intends to start over with the inhabitants of the ark. After the floodwaters recede, God makes a "covenant" (a binding agreement that lasts forever) with Noah (Genesis 8:20-22, 9:8-17). God promises Noah never again to destroy the earth in this way. In other words, God will never again seek to solve the problem of human sinfulness by destroying creation.

This promise, sealed with a rainbow (symbolizing that God was laying down his weapon—his "bow"—for all time) sets up the drama of the biblical narrative. Sin does return. Once again, wickedness covers the earth, and the rebellion of the human race against God crystallizes in building a tower for the purpose of invading heaven and taking control of the universe (Genesis 11:1-9). God puts an end to the rebellious activity and scatters the people across the earth, but still the question remains. How will God act to combat the problem of sin? God has promised not to destroy creation, so he must deal with sin some other way. The covenant with Noah must be kept, but how?

The Patriarchs

Essential Readings: (about Abraham) Genesis 12:1-20; 15:1-18:15; 21:1-7; 22:1-18; (about Jacob) Genesis 25:19-28; 27:1-45; 28:10-22; 32:3-33:17; (about Joseph) Genesis 37:1-36; 39:1-46:7

Genesis 12 to 50 is very different from the first eleven chapters. This section contains stories about Abraham,

Isaac, Jacob, Joseph, and their families. These four men are often called "the Patriarchs." They were the first people chosen by God to enter into a special covenant. In this covenant, God promised to be present with them and their descendants—and bless the whole world through them. The only response God required of them was faith: a commitment to be in relationship with him. This covenant is how God keeps his promise to Noah.

As with Noah, God "starts over" with one person—Abraham. But instead of destroying everybody else, God enters into a relationship with Abraham that will eventually bless "all the families of the earth" (Genesis 12:3). *Covenant,* therefore, is the central concern of Scripture. (The word "testament" means *covenant.* The Old Testament concerns the covenant with Abraham and his descendants, while the New Testament tells how the covenant with Abraham was renewed in Jesus—a direct descendant of Abraham—and reveals how the original covenant was intended to include the whole world.)

If you read about only one patriarch, read about Abraham. Christians, Jews, and Muslims all claim to be children of Abraham. The adherents of these three monotheistic faiths share a common reverence for this patriarch.

In the New Testament letters to the Romans and the Galatians, the apostle Paul exalts Abraham as a paragon of faith who never doubted. The stories about him in Genesis, however, present a much more complicated picture. Here, Abraham (originally named "Abram") is shown as never doubting that God had called him and spoken to him—but often doubting whether God could fulfill his promises. This doubt results in dire consequences when Abram's first son, Ishmael, is born to his servant girl, Hagar. Because Abram and his wife, Sarai, pass into old age without even one child, they choose to take matters into their own hands. In Genesis 16:3, Sarai "gives" Hagar to Abram "as a wife" so that he might have a child. After Ishmael's birth, Sarai's jealousy toward Hagar brings great anguish to Abram's household. (After Ishmael and his mother are expelled from the family, Ishmael becomes the ancestor of the Arabic people, including the Islamic prophet Mohammed.)

Five times (Genesis 12:7; 13:14-15; 15:18-20; 17:5-8; 22:17-18) God renews the covenant with Abraham, each time following some crisis in Abraham's faith. On one of those occasions, God gives "Abram" the name "Abraham," meaning that he will be "the ancestor of a multitude of nations" (Genesis 17:5).

GOD'S COVENANT WITH ABRAHAM (ABRAM)

1. God calls Abram and establishes a covenant—*Genesis 12:1-8*

2. God ratifies the covenant with an ancient ceremony—*Genesis 15:1-21*

3. Abram and Sarai seek to fulfill the covenant on their own—*Genesis 16*

4. God seals the covenant with the sign of circumcision—*Genesis 17:1-22*

5. Isaac is born—*Genesis 21:1-7*

6. God tests Abraham—*Genesis 22:1-19*

Late in life, Sarai miraculously conceives and gives birth to a son, Isaac—the child of promise who signals that God's covenant will indeed be kept. Genesis does not contain a separate cycle of stories about Isaac. But Isaac is important to the overall narrative, especially as the father of Jacob, one of Isaac's twin sons. Jacob inherits the responsibility to pass on the covenant God first made with his grandfather—but not because of any measure of virtue. He is a deeply flawed person who must overcome intense ambition and deceitful behavior. Jacob is renamed "Israel" (which means, somewhat cryptically, "one who wrestles with God") in Genesis 32:22-32. Later, Jacob's sons become the namesakes for the twelve tribes of the nation Israel.

Perhaps the best-told story in Genesis concerns Jacob's eleventh son, Joseph, a brash young dreamer who so rankled his older brothers that they sold him into slavery in Egypt and then told their father he had been mauled to death by a wild animal. Ironically, Joseph rises in Egypt from slavery to become an interpreter of the dreams of Pharaoh (the ruler of Egypt). One of Pharaoh's nightmares portends a terrible famine, but Joseph recognizes from the details of the dream that a time of plenty will come before the famine. Pharaoh rewards Joseph by putting him in charge of a national effort to store all excess grain in preparation. Meanwhile, Joseph's homeland suffers famine. His family migrates to Egypt looking for food, not realizing the official they must petition is Joseph. Joseph toys with this opportunity for revenge on his brothers, but chooses to reconcile with them. Besides making for a good story (and the inspiration for one of Andrew Lloyd Webber's most famous operas), the adventures of Joseph explain how the children of Abraham (called "Hebrews," or migrants) landed in Egypt, where they were eventually forced into slave labor.

The Exodus

Essential Readings: Exodus 1:8-20:21; 24:3-18; 32:1-34:35; 35:4-29; 36:8; 40:34-38

The book of Exodus is largely the story of Moses (another of Abraham's descendants) at a time when those descendants, now called Israelites, were enslaved in Egypt. (This occurred about 1350 years before Christ.) The Pharaoh at the time "did not know Joseph" (Exodus 1:8). He had no appreciation for how that ancestor of the Israelites had benefited Egypt four hundred years earlier. He only knew how great the Israelites' population had become. Fearing they might "join our enemies and fight against us" (Exodus 1:10), Pharaoh enslaved the Israelites and conscripted their men into hard labor so they would be sapped of all strength when they went home to their wives. When the Hebrew population continued to multiply, Pharaoh commanded that all male children born to the Hebrews be killed instantly (Exodus 1:22).

In the midst of this terror, Moses was born. His mother hid him for three months, then placed the child in a basket in the bulrushes of the Nile River. As Moses' sister Miriam watched, the basket floated down the river and was lifted from the water by, of all people, Pharaoh's daughter, who determined to raise the child as her own. Without revealing her relationship to the child, Miriam offered to find a nurse for the baby from among the Hebrew women. The princess agreed, and Miriam brought the baby back to his mother. Later the child was returned to the princess, who gave him the name Moses. So Moses grew up in Egyptian royalty, but also aware of his Hebrew lineage.

As a young adult, Moses sympathized with the plight of his people. One day, he witnessed the beating of one of his kinsmen. Overcome with rage, he murdered the attacker. Knowing he was now a fugitive from Egyptian justice, Moses fled to the wilderness of Midian, where he eventually married and settled down as a shepherd.

Moses' peaceful existence was interrupted when he saw the spectacle of a bush that burned, but would not burn up—an appearance of the God of Abraham (Exodus 3:2). Out of the burning bush, God called Moses to lead the Israelites out of Egypt and into freedom, so that God might renew the covenant. After refuting several objections, God convinced Moses to accept this mission and granted him great powers to break Pharaoh's will and spirit.

Moses led the exodus of the Israelites out of Egypt, across a great semi-desert region called "the wilderness," and eventually back to the land first promised to Abraham. The accounts of Moses' life and the Israelites' adventures in the wilderness, including the giving of the Ten Commandments, are among the Bible's most important stories. Because the New Testament often refers to these events, Christian readers of the Bible need to be familiar with them. Although the Old Testament as a whole can be difficult material for Christians, the book of Genesis and the first 20 chapters of Exodus provide important background. Even if some of this material leaves you troubled or confused, your understanding of the New Testament will be greatly enhanced if you know its basic chronology.

The Law

Essential Readings: Deuteronomy 6:1-25; 10:12-22; 30:1-31:8; 34:1-12

God gave more than the Ten Commandments to Moses. In fact, the entire "Law of Moses" contains 613 commandments. A large portion of the Torah details these regulations stipulated by God for living in the Promised Land. An important teaching of the New Testament is that Christians are not bound to the letter of the Law of Moses. For instance, Christians are not required to follow kosher laws that regulate what foods to eat and how to prepare them. Nor are Christian males required to be circumcised, as the law requires of Jewish males. The major festivals prescribed in the Torah—Passover, the spring and fall harvest festivals, Rosh Hashanah (the Jewish New Year) and Yom Kippur (the Day of Atonement)—are not observed by Christians. Further, none of the laws regarding sacrifices or entrance into the Tabernacle—the Israelites' place of worship—applies to us. So do these laws serve *any* purpose for Christians? Why are they still a part of our Bible?

Many of these same questions have also been asked by Jews for the last 2000 years. At the time of Christ, many Jewish teachers questioned how best to live by the covenant—and a growing number doubted that sacrifices should be at the heart of their faith. The great rabbi Hillel, who taught during the century before Christ, famously said, "That which is hateful to you, do not do to your fellow. That is the whole Torah. The rest is the explanation. Go and learn." Hillel's teachings were among the most influential in formulating all later Jewish teaching.

Not since the Romans destroyed the Jerusalem temple in A.D. 70 have Jews been able to follow any of the laws regarding sacrifice or any of the instructions about the priesthood. Today, different denominations of Jews choose to follow other laws in the Torah more or less strictly. These differences are rooted in disagreements among Jews at the time of Christ's earthly ministry. Before Christianity was a separate religion, it was one of several reform movements within Judaism that were debating how best to carry out the Law of Moses in their own time. Most had come to the conclusion that Israel's emphasis on politics and power (kings and temple priests) had diverted the people from the original purpose of the covenant, which was to live in community with each other and with God. The rabbis of Jesus' time, and Jesus himself, taught that the Law was summed up in just two commandments: "Love the Lord your God with all your heart, soul, mind, and strength" (Deuteronomy 6:5) and "Love your neighbor as yourself" (Leviticus 19:18). (See also Mark 12:28-34.)

So for Christians, the Torah teaches us about the kind of community God desires. Our Christian communities—our churches—are laboratories of covenantal community. God sought this kind of community for Israel over 3000 years ago and still seeks it for the world today. We read the Old Testament, not to discover specific rules to live by, but to uncover the underlying principles of covenantal community that apply to us. That means some parts of the Law of Moses are more important to us than others. How do we make this determination? Christians believe that the teachings and example of Jesus, who said he had not come to "abolish the law ... but to fulfill" (Matthew 5:17), help us to determine the relative importance of not only each part of the Torah, but also of the entire Old Testament.

The Ten Commandments, for instance, are still important to Christians because they provide the broad principles of how to live in community with one another and with God. The first four commandments are about loving God, while the last six address relationships with other people. As we have noted, Jesus emphasized the importance of both loving God and loving neighbor. The Torah also contains clear instructions to take care of the poor, widows, orphans, and non-Israelites (called "strangers" or "aliens") who wander into Israel's territory (Exodus 22:21-22; 23:6, 9; Deuteronomy 10:17-19; 24:14-15, 17-18, 21-22). The Torah demands that laws not be applied in a way that favors one person or class of people over another (Exodus 23:1-2). It even commands that runaway slaves be given refuge (Deuteronomy 23:15-16), which means Israel in 1300 B.C. was more progressive than the United States in

1860! So while many of the rules in the Torah seem archaic and obscure to us, we also find embedded within them the values that are important to God and necessary for any community that seeks to live in covenant with God. In the New Testament, we find Jesus not only affirming these same values, but also encouraging his followers to surpass them with an even higher morality (see Matthew 5:21-48 and Matthew 19:16-22).

History Books

Essential Readings:
> Joshua 24:1-32
> 1 Samuel 3:1-4:1; 8:1-22; 10:17-24; 12:1-25;
>   15:10-31; 16:1-18:16; 31:1-13
> 2 Samuel 5:1-6:5; 6:17-19; 7:1-29; 11:1-12:25
> 1 Kings 2:1-4; 2:10-12; 3:3-15; 4:29-34; 6:1;
>   8:1-21; 9:15-22; 11:1-13; 11:41-43; 12:1-19;
>   17:1-19:15; 19:19-21
> 2 Kings 2:1-25; 4:1-5:19; 17:5-23; 24:1-6;
>   24:10-20; 25:1-21

The Torah is followed by several books (Joshua through Nehemiah, with the exception of Ruth) that contain historical material. The style of writing and the vocabulary indicates they are actually an extension of the book of Deuteronomy. Therefore, scholars refer to them collectively as "the Deuteronomic history," meaning Israel's history from the point of view of the book of Deuteronomy. These books contain many engaging stories that provide insight into the meaning of faith. They also include stories that some might consider too salacious for young children—stories involving violence, sexual intrigue, and political corruption. Through it all, the Deuteronomic history demonstrates how God's purposes are never thwarted, no matter how unfaithful God's people may be.

This section of the Old Testament is not required reading for beginners. In fact, it is not really necessary for a basic understanding of the Christian faith. The gospels record only two occasions when Jesus referred to this historical material. Most New Testament references to the Old Testament are from either the Torah or the prophets (which I will discuss next). Still, the Deuteronomic history relates how people of faith in the past have understood and known God, and they give us valuable insight into Jesus' family history. Those texts I have identified as "essential readings" will afford a good overview of that history. As I sum up the Deuteronomic history below, I will note the points that are most relevant to Christianity.

The book of *Joshua* recounts how the Israelites claimed the land of Canaan as the land of Israel first promised to Abraham. Following Moses' death, Joshua succeeded him as Israel's leader and proved to be an effective warrior. Under his leadership, Israel defeated a total of 31 kings in battle, and all their cities fell under Israelite control. The first half of Joshua describes this conquest. The last half spells out how the land was apportioned to each of the twelve tribes of Israel.

The book of *Judges* is named for the way Israel governed itself once it had settled the Promised Land. According to God's instructions in Deuteronomy 16:18, the nation was divided into twelve tribes, each ruled by a judge who was both a military leader and a settler of disputes. This form of government, which lacked a central ruling authority such as a king, would have been very unusual in the ancient world. Israel was a *theocracy*—meaning they were ruled directly by God. While all the neighboring nations were ruled by kings, Israel claimed God as its king. The book of Judges, however, tells how the people of Israel suffered from a growing moral anarchy—summed up in the last verse of the book, which says, "all the people did what was right in their own eyes."

The reader notices a cyclical pattern to the stories. The Israelites "did what was evil in the sight of the Lord." Then, the Israelites "cried out for help," and God answered by raising up a judge to deliver them. But after each of these judges drove back Israel's enemies, "the Israelites again did what was evil in the sight of the Lord." The repeated cycle of events reveals two things. First, the people are not living according to the covenant. Second, God never wavers in faithfulness to the people, no matter how many times they ignore the covenant.

The period of the Judges came to an end when the Israelites determined that they needed a king to centralize their nation and raise an army strong enough to defend themselves against emerging world powers. The book of *1 Samuel* begins with the story of one judge, Samuel, who was so widely respected that he became the judge of all Israel and functioned very much like a king. During Samuel's judgeship, the Israelites were not only faithful to the covenant, but were also protected from their enemies.

When Samuel grew old, the people demanded a king. Samuel's sons were weak leaders, and the Israelites feared that unless they established a strong monarchy, they would fall onto hard times. They pled with Samuel to express this desire to God in their behalf. A monarchy, however, was not in God's plan. God told Samuel to warn the people that giving so much power to one person would only invite corruption, and would cause the people to trust more in political power than in divine protection. Still, the people persisted, and in the end, God granted their request. Israel became a kingdom about 1000 years before the time of Christ.

A large portion of the Deuteronomic history, from *1 Samuel 8* to *1 Kings 11*, tells the story of the only three kings who ruled over all Israel: Saul, David, and Solomon. Saul began his reign with great promise, but then became a tragic disappointment. David, something of a guerrilla fighter who gained fame for his unlikely defeat of Goliath, a leader of the Philistines, succeeded Saul. (The familiar story of David and Goliath is recorded in 1 Samuel 17.) Under David, Israel flourished and eventually became the most powerful nation on earth. Because of this, and because he ruled Israel with "justice and equity for all the people" (2 Samuel 8:15), future generations of Israelites remembered David as an ideal king. During the time of Jesus, many Jews believed that God would save the people from their oppressors by raising up a new king from the lineage of David. Some believed this "son of David" would be an earthly king who would restore Israel to her former glory. Others believed he would be a spiritual king who would rule over a new heavenly order. In the New Testament, the gospel writers and the apostle Paul attest that

Jesus was a direct descendent of David (Luke 1:32, Romans 1:3) and some of Jesus' admirers called him "Son of David" (Matthew 9:27, 12:23, 15:22, 20:30, 21:9).

Following David's death, Israel's prosperity continued during the reign of his son, Solomon. But Solomon, for all his wisdom, was corrupt and ruthless. He used slave labor to build the temple in the capital city of Jerusalem, a tragic irony for a people once freed from slavery by the hand of God. He also over-taxed every tribe except his own, Judah. Upon his death, ten of the twelve tribes of Israel petitioned Solomon's son Rehoboam to reverse his father's harsh policies. When he refused, the ten tribes seceded to form their own nation.

For the next 200 years, Israel existed as a divided kingdom—two nations weakened in power and vulnerable to invasion. The northern kingdom retained the name "Israel," while the southern kingdom was known as "Judah," since most of that kingdom consisted of the territory of the tribe of Judah. *1 Kings 12* to *2 Kings 25* tells the story of these divided kingdoms and provides a summary judgment of each king who ruled over Israel or Judah. It is telling that twice as many kings "did what was evil in the sight of the Lord" than "did what was right in the sight of the Lord." The Deuteronomic history reveals that God's original warnings about kingship all proved true.

Within this section of the Bible we find the stories of Israel's first great prophet, Elijah, and his protégé, Elisha. Knowing about these two prophets is important for reading the New Testament. In a contest on Mt. Carmel, Elijah proved that the God of Israel was more powerful than the

Canaanite gods. He not only publicly criticized the king of Israel and his wife, Jezebel, but is also credited with many miracles, including raising a child from the dead. In the gospels, Elijah is heralded as one of the principle authorities within Judaism. Jesus associated him with John the Baptist, the one who announced Jesus' coming and was imprisoned just before Jesus began his public ministry (see Matthew 11:11-14 and 17:10-12). Some of the people of Galilee speculated that Jesus might in fact represent the return of Elijah. In his teachings, Jesus referred to both Elijah and Elisha.

The history of kingship ended in disaster. The Assyrian Empire destroyed the northern kingdom about 700 years before Christ. The southern kingdom lasted longer, but it was eventually shattered by the Babylonians (ancestors of present-day Iraq) some 600 years before Christ. The book of 2 Kings concludes with the tragic account of how the Babylonians burned Solomon's temple to the ground and carried into exile most of the people of Judah, while leaving the "poorest of the poor" to survive amid the smoldering rubble of Jerusalem.

While both the southern and northern kingdoms were destroyed, their fates were quite different. Citizens of the northern kingdom were simply expelled from their home-land. They dispersed all over the Middle East, never to be rejoined as the ten tribes they once were. Most of the citizens of the southern kingdom, on the other hand, remained intact, because they were forcibly exiled to Babylon.

The Deuteronomic history reveals the complete failure of a centralized monarchy to lead the nation in practicing the covenantal community envisioned in the Torah. Even David, the greatest and most fondly remembered of all the kings, is shown to be of questionable moral character. 2 Samuel 11-12 tells the story of David's adulterous affair with Bathsheba. The narrative implies that this relationship was not consensual. ("David sent messengers to fetch her" [2 Samuel 11:4].) When Bathsheba became pregnant with David's child, David ordered Bathsheba's husband, a general in the Israelite army, moved to the front lines of battle, where he was quickly killed. Through the prophet Nathan, God condemned David for his behavior. While God remained true to an earlier promise to bless David's lineage, David himself suffered agony in his personal life. The child born to Bathsheba died. One of his sons committed incest against one of his daughters, tearing the family apart. Eventually, David's first-born son Absalom mounted an unsuccessful coup against his father that resulted in Absalom's death. David died heartbroken.

The Old Testament also contains another version of the same history, told from the perspective of the tribe of Judah following the exile. *1 and 2 Chronicles* borrow heavily from the Deuteronomic history but cast the monarchy and the temple in a much better light. David and Solomon's worst indiscretions are removed from the story. They are both presented as ideal kings. After reporting the secession of the northern tribes, Chronicles follows only the history of the southern kingdom of Judah. This record doesn't end with the exile, but picks up again in the books of *Ezra* and *Nehemiah* with the rebuilding of the temple and the city of

The skyline of Jerusalem today. The most prominent feature, the Dome of the Rock, is a Muslim holy site that sits on the exact spot where the Holy of Holies inside the Jewish temple once stood. The large open area around the Dome of the Rock is still known as "the Temple Mount." Jews, Muslims, and Christians also revere this location as the site of Abraham's near-sacrifice of his son Isaac.

Orthodox Jews pray at the Western Wall, the only portion of the Jerusalem temple still standing.

Jerusalem after the exile. It records events until about 400 years before Christ.

The different points of view represented in these two versions of Israel's history reflect the great debate that would remain at the center of Jewish life into the time of Christ. Should the people of God seek to restore the kingdom of David and the Jerusalem priesthood—or forsake these powerful institutions and focus instead on living in covenantal community? To find the answer, many of the Jewish people turned to the words of the prophets.

The Prophets

Essential Readings:
>Jeremiah 23:1-8; 25:1-14; 29:1-14; 31:31-34
>Ezekiel 34:1-31; 37:1-14
>Isaiah 9:1-7; 11:1-9; 40:1-5; 27-31; 52:13-53:12;
>   60:1-3; 61:1-2

Fifteen of the books in the Old Testament contain sermons, writings, and stories of the Hebrew prophets. The prophets were unusual people who claimed to speak for God. In their own time, they were often rejected because they were highly critical of the hypocrisy and social injustice of the Israelites and warned of God's judgment if behavior did not change. When later events, like the destruction of the northern kingdom and the Babylonian exile, came to pass, these prophets were seen in retrospect as having spoken for God. Their sermons, which had been written down by their followers, were collected and eventually added to the Hebrew Scriptures.

The prophetic writings are not arranged chronologically. The books of the "major" prophets—Isaiah, Jeremiah, and Ezekiel—come first. These prophets are the most revered. The last twelve books of the Old Testament, Daniel through Malachi, contain sermons of "minor" prophets. The earliest of these prophets, Amos, lived about 750 years before Christ. It is difficult to say which prophet came last, though several of the minor prophets probably preached about 400 years before Christ.

The Babylonian exile was a pivotal moment in the history of the Israelites, who now referred to themselves as "Jews," since those taken into exile were all members of the tribe of Judah. Like the covenant with Abraham and the Exodus, this event was of monumental importance for Jewish history. During the exile, many people thought God had abandoned them. They could not understand why God was not answering their prayers. Why didn't God deliver them the way God had freed their ancestors from Egyptian slavery? Prophets arose among the exiled Jews to answer that question, and the Jewish understanding of God deepened. Jews became strict "monotheists," believing in the existence of only one God who created the entire world. This theology was critical for coping with the exile, for it meant that God was the God of all people, not just Jews. God was just as present in Babylon as in Jerusalem and just as concerned for the Babylonians as for the Jews.

Since the historical material of the Old Testament does not include details about the exile, most of our information about this important period comes from those prophets who lived at that time. Jeremiah was advising the kings of

Judah just before the Babylonians invaded Jerusalem. He and his followers managed to escape Jerusalem just before the destruction of the temple and fled to Egypt. From there, he sent letters to the Jews living in Babylon, encouraging them to go on with their lives, knowing that God would still be present with them (Jeremiah 29:1-14). The prophet Ezekiel ministered to his fellow Jews in Babylon, sharing visions of an eventual return to the Promised Land and the rebuilding of the temple. One famous text from Ezekiel pictures Israel as a valley of dry bones that God raises to new life (Ezekiel 37:1-14).

EXILE IN BABYLON

1. A Prophet Warns of Destruction—*Jeremiah 6:13-30*

2. Babylon Destroys Jerusalem—*2 Kings 25:1-21*

3. The People Weep in Exile—*Psalms 80 and 137*

4. A Prophet Gives Counsel to Those Living in Exile—*Jeremiah 29:1-14*

5. A Prophet Comforts the People—*Isaiah 40:1-5, 27-31*

Another prophet during the exile was an anonymous one whose preaching is contained in Isaiah chapters 40-55. (Isaiah, unlike most of the prophetic books, is an anthology of sermons delivered over a period of roughly 300 years by several prophets in the same tradition.) These chapters contain many passages that early Christians would find important for understanding Jesus.

It will be helpful to read Isaiah chapter 40 and chapter 53. Chapter 40 tells the exiled Jews that God is the Creator of the whole world and therefore exists everywhere, even in Babylon. Note particularly verses 27-28, in which the prophet quotes the laments of the exiled Jews and then gives them hope by declaring that God is the "Creator of the ends of the earth." Chapter 53 speaks of a servant of God who will suffer for the sake of others. In all likelihood, the prophet was speaking of Israel, explaining why the Jews had been allowed to suffer for so long, even though they were God's people. Centuries later, early Christians would come to believe that Jesus himself embodied this vision, suffering on the cross for the sake of the world. Jesus, therefore, embodied Israel. His life, death, and resurrection fulfilled the purpose and promise of Israel. For this reason, two of the gospels contain genealogies of Jesus' family that show that he was a direct descendent of both Abraham and David, and a member of the tribe of Judah.

The prophets were important not only for the hope they gave to those in exile, but also for how they interpreted the meaning of the exile. All three major prophets agreed that the exile resulted from Israel's lack of faithfulness to the covenant. They spoke critically of the way the kings of both Israel and Judah had led God's people astray. Both major and minor prophets spoke powerfully about the hypocrisy of observing the letter of the law and keeping all the prescribed festivals, while ignoring the plight of the poor and other disadvantaged groups in Israelite society. Many of the prophets' sermons centered on the need for justice and righteousness and named these values as more important than correct sacrifices in the temple. (For examples, see Isaiah 1:12-20; Hosea 6:4-6; Amos 5:21-24; and Micah 6:6-8.) The same sentiment was also expressed by Jesus (Matthew 9:13; 12:7).

Israel's greatest prophets lived before and during the exile. Other prophets whose sermons are contained in the Old Testament lived after the exile. Because of unfolding historical events, their words were eventually recognized to be God-given as well. Many people think of prophets as people who predict the future, but this is not really correct. Prophets were people who shared God's vision. They could see the world as God saw it—and so could tell people what God was calling them to do. They were keenly aware of the dangers that lay ahead for those who disobeyed God, as well as the rewards awaiting those who were faithful to God. Therefore, they often spoke of how God might be involved in future events. Because they displayed penetrating political as well as spiritual insight, what they said was fulfilled by future history.

Other Writings

The rest of the Old Testament—*Ruth, Esther* through *the Song of Solomon,* and *Lamentations*—are books that do not fit neatly into any category. These books address deep philosophical questions, tell popular stories, and preserve poetry. One book that is particularly important for Christians is *Psalms*, the collection of 150 songs used by the Israelites, and later by the early Christians, in their worship services. If you followed my advice in chapter 1, you are already familiar with at least some of the psalms.

Now, with more understanding of the history of the people of Israel, you will want to read them again.

The psalms were composed over a long period. Some date to the time of King David, others to the Babylonian exile or later. The collection is divided into five clearly demarcated books, corresponding to the five books of the Torah. Seventy-three of them are called "Psalms of David." According to 1 Samuel 16:14-23, 2 Samuel 1:17-27, and 2 Samuel 22:1-51, David was a poet and a musician. Some of the psalms relate closely to events in his life. He may have composed others after he became king to use in temple worship. As king, David also appointed hymn-writers. Later kings continued this tradition, so it is possible that some of the "Psalms of David" were written in later generations in the tradition of David.

The psalms are valuable because they give us insight into ancient Israel, but their primary value is in guiding God's people in prayer and worship. With the possible exception of the book of Isaiah, no biblical book was more frequently consulted by early Christians.

The Old Testament and the Jewish Bible

The 39 books common to all Christian editions of the Old Testament are the same ones found in the Jewish Bible, though not in the same order. The order that is found in Christian Bibles first existed in a Greek translation of these writings known as the "Septuagint." The name means "seventy" and refers to a group of seventy scholars who apparently translated all this material from Hebrew into Greek around 200 years before the birth of Christ. Since

Greek was fast becoming the language of the international marketplace, much the way English functions today, it seemed prudent to provide a Greek translation of the Jewish Scriptures so that Jews living in every part of the world could read them.

The Septuagint, however, did not stop with translating the texts that all Jews considered Scripture. It included the historical material, the preaching of many prophets, and a number of other writings that were popular among Jews of that time. Most of these books were treated like Scripture but were not officially recognized by the ruling authorities of Judaism. Not until A.D. 80 did a special council of Jewish leaders adopt most of them as the Jewish Bible, arranging them according to three categories—the Law (*Torah*), the Prophets (*Nevi'im*), and the Writings (*Kethuvim*), together known as the "Tanakh" (an acronym for the three sections using the Hebrew equivalents of "T," "N," and "K.") The Tanakh required a reordering of the books in the Septuagint, but by the time that decision was made, Christians had already begun using the Septuagint as it was originally organized.

The difference in how the Jewish Bible and Christian Old Testament order the books is significant. Particularly interesting is the way each collection ends. The last book in the Jewish Tanakh is 2 Chronicles, which ends with the exhortation for the Jewish people to "go up" to the city of Jerusalem. The Christian Old Testament ends with the prophet Malachi proclaiming God's promise to send the prophet Elijah "before the great and terrible day of the Lord comes. He will turn the hearts of parents to their children and the hearts of children to their parents, so that I will not come and strike the land with a curse." This promise appears again in Luke 1:17, when an angel announces the coming birth of John the Baptist. "With the spirit and power of Elijah he will go before [the Lord] to turn the hearts of parents to their children, and the disobedient to the wisdom of the righteous, to make ready a people prepared for the Lord." Jesus later taught that Elijah had already returned in the person of John the Baptist (Matthew 17:10-12).

The Apocrypha

Some editions of the Bible also contain fifteen books that are collectively known as the "Apocrypha." None of these books was ever considered part of the Hebrew canon, but all were popular among the Jewish people around the time of Christ, and had been included as part of the Septuagint. By the time Jerome translated the Bible into Latin some 600 years later, several highly regarded Christian scholars had begun to make a distinction between these fifteen books and the Hebrew Scriptures.

Jerome included them in his Latin translation, but added a preface explaining that they were "apocryphal" works to be considered separate from the rest of the Bible. Later copyists of Jerome's Vulgate failed to include this preface, and by the Middle Ages, the Apocrypha was considered as much Scripture as the other books of the Bible.

In the sixteenth century, Protestant reformers separated the books of the Apocrypha from the Old Testament, but continued to include them as an appendix to the Scriptures.

The first reformer, Martin Luther, wrote in the preface of his translation that they were "good and useful to be read." In the sixteenth century, the Church of England regarded the Apocrypha as valuable for "example of life and instruction of manners" but not for the establishment of any doctrine. In many Protestant circles today, the Apocrypha has been removed from the Bible altogether, while Roman Catholics and Eastern Orthodox Christians continue to regard the Apocrypha as Scripture.

The word "apocrypha" means "hidden." Before Christianity began, Jewish scholars debated the value of these books. Some argued that they were hidden because they contained mysterious, profound truth that most people could not understand. Other scholars derided them as needing to be hidden because they contained heresy and should not be read. From its beginning, the role of the Apocrypha has been in dispute.

Though most Protestants today do not include the Apocrypha among the books of the Bible, some of its books still have value for all Christians. The books of 1 and 2 Maccabees contain important historical material about the Jews from about 350 to164 B.C., climaxing with the story of the Jews, under the leadership of Judas Maccabeus, defeating the Greek army and purifying the temple—an event commemorated in the Jewish festival of Hannukah. Another apocryphal book, 2 Esdras, is an example of "apocalyptic" literature (which I will discuss more fully in the section on the New Testament). Reading 2 Esdras can deepen our understanding of other apocalyptic material in the Bible. The Apocrypha also contains delightful stories from Jewish folklore that, while not authoritative for us, have value in their own right.

Still, the study of the Apocrypha is peripheral to the study of the Bible. It can illuminate the meaning of some texts in the Bible, but it is not at all necessary for comprehending God's Word to us.

The Hebrew Scriptures as Part of the Christian Bible

Earlier I commented on why the Torah is important to Christians. But what about the rest of the Old Testament? It is a huge amount of material—nearly four times the length of the New Testament. Wouldn't it have made sense to select only portions of the Hebrew Scriptures—the ones most applicable to the Christian faith—to include in the Christian Bible?

Clearly not all of the Old Testament holds equal importance for Christians (or Jews, for that matter). If, as Jesus and other ancient rabbis said, the greatest commandment is to love God with all your being, and the second is to love your neighbor as you love yourself, then certain texts—those that increase our understanding of how to love God and neighbor—will have more importance. In the same way, those Old Testament stories specifically mentioned in the New Testament hold greater importance for Christians than those that are never referenced. And the words of those prophets quoted by Jesus and the New Testament writers are understandably of more interest to Christians than those whose words are never mentioned.

Still, it is important that Christians recognize all of the Old Testament as part of our Bible for the simple reason that we cannot understand the "new" testament (or New Covenant) unless we know the "old" covenant on which it is based. Jesus never recanted the Jewish religion, nor did the early Christians. For the first 50 years after the resurrection of Jesus, Christianity was a movement within Judaism. The Jewish Bible was the *only* Bible the church had during this period of time.

As our overview of the New Testament will show, it was the inclusion of non-Jews into the Christian movement that eventually led to it becoming a separate religion. Yet even after Christianity became predominantly non-Jewish, church leaders continued to insist that the Hebrew Bible was part of the Christian Bible—if for no other reason than it was Jesus' Bible. The letter of the Jewish law is not binding on Christians. But the Torah is still the Word of God for Christians, because through the Torah we learn about God's relationship to us. God also continues to speak to us through the experiences of the many men and women whose stories are told in the history books. Further, many of the words of the prophets are as relevant today as they were then, particularly on issues of social justice.

On the other hand, it is important to recognize that the Old Testament serves a different purpose for Christians than for Jews. If we were Jews, we would probably spend most of our study time in the Torah, seeking to understand how to apply each law—in spirit if not in letter—to our own lives. For Christians, the Old Testament points toward Christ. For us, Christ stands at the center of all Scripture. His teachings help us determine the relative importance of every other part of the Bible. His death and resurrection displace the exodus as the central event of Scripture. (In fact, Jesus spoke of his death and resurrection as a *new* exodus accomplishing a *new* covenant.) So for Christians, the primary focus of Bible study should be the New Testament, and specifically, the gospels.

The city of Tiberius, built during Jesus' lifetime,
on the Sea of Galilee, also known as Lake Genneserat and
the Sea of Tiberias. Much of Jesus' public ministry took
place along the northern shore visible in this picture.

CHAPTER 3

THE NEW TESTAMENT

THE NEW TESTAMENT (or better, "New Covenant") is a collection of writings that address how God has renewed the covenants of the Old Testament in the person of Jesus of Nazareth, the Messiah and the Son of God. Just as the earlier covenants revealed how God was redeeming the world and restoring humanity's relationship to God and neighbor, so this covenant is God's way of forming new communities that teach and practice the values central to God's reign over creation.

This covenant, however, is distinct from those described in the Old Testament because it is centered in the life, death, and resurrection of one human being who not only taught about God's reign, but also embodied it fully himself. Furthermore, when he was crucified by earthly powers that considered him a threat, God raised him from the dead, and he eventually ascended to heaven so that he could be spiritually present with all those who gather in his name. The

New Covenant is more than a new set of guidelines for how to be a community in covenant with God and one another. It is the promise of the real presence of the risen Jesus to give life and spirit to such communities, and to personally fulfill God's dreams for all creation at the end of time.

As you read the New Testament, you will come across several words and phrases used to describe Jesus. These titles are common in Christian parlance, but are not always defined. For instance, the New Testament contains hundreds of references to Jesus as "Messiah," a Hebrew term that means, "anointed one." ("Christ" is the Greek equivalent of "Messiah.") Originally, this term applied to kings of Israel and Judah who were anointed with oil as a sign of God's blessing. Following the exile in Babylon, "Messiah" took on greater meaning. As I noted earlier, the Jewish people hoped for a new king in the line of David to save them from the suffering they endured at the hands of foreign powers. Such a savior would have to be more than an ordinary king, even one as great as David. There was little consensus, however, about the exact nature of the coming Messiah. By the time of Jesus' birth, "Messiah" meant everything from king to warrior to angel. Christians believe that the true nature of the Messiah is revealed in the life and ministry of Jesus.

The New Testament also calls Jesus "Son of God," a title that, like "Messiah," was given to kings of Israel and Judah. For early Christians, however, Jesus as "Son of God" expressed how he perfectly revealed the nature of God. That is, Jesus was of the same essence as God. In John 14:7, Jesus said, "If you know me, you will know my Father also."

Jesus is also called "Savior," a term used in the Greek-speaking world to refer to Greco-Roman gods who were believed to bring healing to those who suffered. In Jewish culture, it referred to "wholeness" or "full health." The New Testament presents Jesus as one who saves us from our sins and the sins of the world (Matthew 1:21). By doing so, Jesus makes us whole. Because sin is alienation from God, Jesus' salvation is reconciliation to God (2 Corinthians 5:18-19).

The first four books of the New Testament are called "gospels." "Gospel" comes from an Old English word, "Goodspell," which means "good news." It translates the Greek word *euangellion*, which also means "good news." This word appears several times in the New Testament and refers to the proclamation that Jesus is the Savior of the world. It also refers to a particular kind of literature that selects certain stories and teachings of Jesus to demonstrate *how* he is the Savior of the world.

We know from historical records that Jesus of Nazareth died by execution on a Roman cross about A.D. 30. We also know that his followers presented a threat to the Roman Empire for a variety of reasons, leading to their frequent persecution for the next 300 years. Beyond these sketchy details, the gospels are the only records we have about Jesus. The earliest gospel is Mark, probably written around A.D. 65. Until that time, all the original disciples of Jesus (except for Judas, who committed suicide after betraying Jesus) were alive and serving as traveling missionaries, telling their favorite stories about Jesus. But in the year 64, the Roman Emperor Nero, who hated the Christians, blamed them for burning the city of Rome and ordered their arrest. Many were fed to the lions in the Roman Coliseum for the entertainment of Rome's citizens. The leaders of the church, including most or all of the disciples, were executed by crucifixion or beheading.

With all the original eyewitnesses to Jesus now dead, the early church faced a crisis. To prevent the stories and sayings of Jesus from being lost, scribes began writing them down. Many of these writings circulated as disconnected anecdotes and quotations. Mark was the first to put these memories into a narrative form and to fashion his story of Jesus as a teaching tool for Christians. Other Christians attempted similar gospels, and by the early 100s, the church's leaders saw the need to settle on which gospels would be considered reliable witnesses to Jesus, so as to prevent the spread of false teachings that might lead to the development of faulty doctrine.

Four were chosen: *Matthew, Mark, Luke,* and *John.* The first three are integrally related: Matthew and Luke both used Mark as a source and added other material. Matthew and Luke also shared an additional source of teaching material that Mark apparently did not know about. Although each of these three gospels has its own perspective on the nature of Jesus and the purpose of his ministry, they share a general chronology of events in Jesus' life, and are called the "synoptic" gospels. (*Syn-optic* means "of the same eye.") John, on the other hand, is quite different. The fourth gospel probably developed over a long period of time, and contains several layers of tradition about Jesus. Some of John is eyewitness material, while some of it reflects later teaching about Jesus. In some ways, John is easier to read than the synoptic gospels. His language is simple, even repetitive. But in another way, John is more difficult to grasp, because it is written with different layers of meaning and is full of symbolism.

Why did the early church choose these four gospels and not others? The main reason is probably "apostolicity," an effort to retain the witness of the first apostles of Jesus. ("Apostles" is a term used to describe Jesus' twelve disciples. An apostle is one who is "sent out.") The most important test any writing had to pass to be included in the New Testament was whether it was consistent with the teachings of the apostles. The four gospels indicate that four different apostolic traditions remained intact into the second Christian century, and the rest of the New Testament has links to one of these four traditions.

The gospel of Matthew traces back to the apostle Matthew, also called Levi. Most scholars today believe that this gospel, like John, developed over a period of time— roughly 30 years—in a "Matthean school." The gospel is full of references to Jewish scripture and culture, indicating that it was written for Jewish-Christians living in Palestine, in and around Jerusalem. The letter to the Hebrews and the letter of James were likewise written to Jewish-Christians, indicating that they might also belong to the Matthew tradition.

Mark was a disciple of Peter, so the second gospel is thought to represent the tradition of Peter, who may have founded the church in Rome. This gospel was probably written with the purpose of encouraging Roman Christians suffering through Nero's persecution. Two letters in the New Testament are also associated by name with Peter, and the little letter of Jude depends on 2 Peter for some of its contents.

Luke was a traveling companion of the apostle Paul, who was not among the original twelve but, for reasons I shall discuss shortly, was granted the status of apostle by the early church. The tradition of Paul is the most dominant in the New Testament. *The Acts of the Apostles* is actually a second volume of the gospel of Luke, and thirteen letters are associated with Paul. This means that two-thirds of the New Testament reflects the Pauline tradition.

John, the Beloved Disciple, the son of Zebedee, is probably the earliest contributor to the gospel of John, as well as the founder of a community of Christians somewhere in Asia Minor that continued after his death. This community was led by "elders" who probably authored the letters of 1, 2, and 3 John and the book of Revelation. The relationship of these five books is indisputable, since all use imagery and language found nowhere else in the New Testament.

As the preceding paragraphs indicate, one way to divide the New Testament is according to apostolic traditions. However, when the church finally settled on the contents of the New Testament in the early fifth century, the books were arranged according to *genre*. Basically, there are two genres in the New Testament. The first is *narrative*, or story material. It consists of the four gospels and Acts, and makes up about 60 percent of the New Testament. The other 40 percent consists of 22 *epistles*, or letters. The first nine epistles, *Romans* through *2 Thessalonians*, arranged in order from longest to shortest, are written by Paul to church congregations. The next four, *1 and 2 Timothy, Titus,* and *Philemon,* are addressed to individuals. The next eight, *Hebrews* through *Jude*, are called "General Epistles" because they speak in general terms to the whole church. The General Epistles have multiple authors. The last book, *The Revelation*, stands in a category by itself. It belongs to a genre called "apocalyptic" (the book's title in Greek is

Apocalypsis), which uses rich symbolism to convey visions about the end of time. Still, the Revelation is self-described as an epistle to "the seven churches that are in Asia."

The oldest material in the New Testament was written by Paul. His letters to the Thessalonians, the earliest ones we have, date to around A.D. 50. All of Paul's letters had to have been written before 64, when Paul was beheaded by Nero. Hebrews and James may have been written in the 60s or early 70s. The gospels were completed between the years 65 and 95, and the other New Testament writings were written anywhere from 65 to 120.

One controversy in New Testament studies has to do with the authorship of some of the epistles. In the ancient world, it was common for people to write using someone else's name, a practice called "pseudonomy." This practice was not deceitful. The people whose names were assumed had already died, and everyone knew they couldn't be the authors of those texts. It was actually a form of humility for writers of the early church not to take credit for their writings but to stand in the tradition of another revered leader. In the New Testament, there may be as many as eight pseudonymous texts. It is widely believed that Paul did not write 1 Timothy or Titus, because they reflect a level of church organization that was not present in the time of Paul, and because the linguistic style is so different from Paul's other epistles. The letters of Ephesians, Colossians, 2 Thessalonians, and 2 Timothy are also held by some scholars to be pseudonymous, though there is much less consensus. 1 Peter is generally assumed to be a second-century composition, and 2 Peter may also be pseudonymous, though the evidence is less convincing. 1, 2, and 3 John were probably not written by John the apostle, but that would not make them pseudonymous, since the author never identifies himself in the text. Titles were attached to the various books long after they were written.

Issues of authorship become important for advanced study of the New Testament, but need not concern a beginning reader. As with the Old Testament, the primary purpose of these books is to invite us into relationship with God. The central message about this relationship in the New Testament is that in Jesus Christ, God became one with us. Though he was killed, he was raised from the dead and now lives among us. So it is through the risen Christ that God comes to us, and even dwells within us.

The Gospels

Essential Readings: One "synoptic" gospel; John 1:1-14; 6:1-69; 13:31-15:17

Where is the best place to begin reading about Jesus? Which gospel is the best to start with? That question is difficult to answer. A strong case can be made that Matthew is the place to begin, because it is the first book, and therefore the early church intended it to be read first. Many of Jesus' most familiar teachings are found here, including the Beatitudes (5:1-12), the Lord's Prayer (6:9-13) and the Golden Rule (7:12). Matthew uses most of Mark's gospel and adds a lot of teaching material. This gospel is arranged very neatly into a prologue, five books, and the story of the crucifixion and resurrection. The five books in the middle all contain a section of stories and a section of teaching.

If you are mostly interested in Jesus' *teaching*, Matthew is probably the best gospel to read first. Mark might be the better choice because of its brevity, which should not be taken as a lack of profundity. The way Mark tells the story of Jesus is breathtaking, especially considering that his audience was people in the midst of persecution. Mark shows how the persecution of Christians in his time is actually a participation in the crucifixion of Jesus. In both Jesus' time and the church's, the same forces of evil seek to destroy the gospel. But just as they failed in Jesus' time, so they will fail now. Mark's gospel is more apocalyptic than the other three, which will appeal to some readers.

MAJOR EVENTS IN THE LIFE OF JESUS

1. **Birth**—*Matthew 1:18-2:18; Luke 2:1-20*

2. **Baptism**—*Matthew 3:1-17; Mark 1:4-11; Luke 3:1-22* *

3. **Temptation**—*Matthew 4:1-17; Luke 4:1-15* *

4. **Feeding of Five Thousand**—*Matthew 14:13-21; Mark 6:30-44; Luke 9:10-17; John 6:1-13*

5. **The Transfiguration**—*Matthew 17:1-8; Mark 9:2-8; Luke 9:28-36* *

6. **Entry into Jerusalem**—*Matthew 21:1-9; Mark 11:1-11; Luke 19:28-38; John 12:12-19*

7. **The Last Supper**—*Matthew 26:17-35; Mark 14:12-25; Luke 22:7-38; John 13:1-30* *

8. **Death and Resurrection**—*Matthew 26:30-28:20; Mark 14:26-16:8; Luke 22:39-24:52; John 17:1-21:25* *

* *Can you identify allusions to the Old Testament in these stories?*

The case can also be made for reading Luke first because most of us are probably more like Luke's audience than that of the other three gospels. Luke tells the story of Jesus to convince Gentiles (non-Jews) that he is the Messiah for the world. The theme of a "universal" gospel pervades Luke. (It is hinted at in Matthew and Mark, but obvious in Luke.) Luke also contains some of the church's most beloved stories not found anywhere else, such as the story of shepherds coming to see Jesus at his birth (2:8-20) and Jesus' parable of the prodigal son (15:11-32). If you are most interested in how Jesus came for the whole world and how he showed a special interest in the poor, the sick, women, and others who were overlooked by the world, then begin by reading Luke.

The fifth book in the New Testament, The Acts of the Apostles (or simply Acts), is a second volume of the gospel of Luke, who carries the story of Jesus into the life of the early church. Here we learn of the miracle of Pentecost (Acts 2:1-21), when Jesus' disciples received the Holy Spirit in Jerusalem and were given the miraculous ability to speak the gospel in many tongues. From there, the gospel spreads quickly across Judea, into Syria, and—largely because of Paul's three missionary journeys—all across the Roman Empire. If you choose to read Luke, you might want to continue reading his account to see how the gospel spreads from Jerusalem to Rome.

John presents an interesting dilemma. It would be a mistake to read only John and form one's whole impression of Jesus on the basis of this gospel. You would be equally remiss in not reading any of John along with at least one of the synoptic gospels. One simple way to distinguish between John and the synoptics is that the first three gospels focus on *what Jesus did*, while John focuses on *who Jesus is*. Only in John does Jesus frequently talk about himself in the first person, saying things like "I am the bread of life," "I and the Father are one," and "I am the way, the truth, and the life."

The fourth gospel divides into two sections. Chapters 1 to 11 center around seven miracle stories. Two of these are unique to John: the changing of water to wine and the raising of Lazarus from the dead. Each miracle is a "sign" that reveals how God is present in Jesus. In John 6:1-14, Jesus feeds 5,000 with five loaves of bread and two fish. This story is found in all four gospels, but only in John does Jesus say, "I am the bread of life." In the healing of the blind man, Jesus says, "I am the light of the world." Just before raising Lazarus, he says, "I am the resurrection and the life."

John chapters 12 to 21 focus on the death and resurrection of Jesus. In the other gospels, these events receive only a third to a half as much attention. John tells the story in far greater detail. He credits Jesus with long speeches and prayers, not just short parables and single-sentence quotes. Some of these sayings are indispensable to the church's later creeds about the nature of God as Father, Son, and Holy Spirit.

TEACHINGS OF JESUS

1. "Sermon on the Mount"—*Matthew 5:1-7:29**
2. Parables—*Matthew 13:1-58; 21:33-22:10; 25:1-46; Luke 15:1-32*
3. "The Bread of Life"—*John 6:14-71**
4. "The New Commandment"—*John 13:31-15:27*

*Can you identify allusions to the Old Testament in these texts?

Despite the many differences among the four gospels, they share some basic similarities. All four report Jesus' baptism by John the Baptist, who had proclaimed the coming of the Messiah. All four tell of Jesus driving the moneychangers out of the Jerusalem temple and claiming it as a house of prayer to God. The story of Jesus feeding five thousand with five loaves of bread and two fish is common to all four gospels. Several events of the final week of Jesus' earthly ministry are also found in all the gospels: his entrance into Jerusalem to shouts of "Hosanna!"; a meal with his disciples; Judas' betrayal and Peter's denial of Jesus; Jesus' trial before the Jewish high priest; another trial before the Roman Procurator Pontius Pilate; his crucifixion; and his resurrection.

If you are motivated enough, read all four gospels from start to finish, noting the similarities and differences. If you want to start on a smaller scale, pick one of the synoptic gospels, and supplement it by reading John 1:1-14; 6:1-69; and 13:31-15:17.

THE GOSPELS AND HISTORY

Having read the gospels, you might be tempted to ask, "Can I trust what I have read? How do we know this is what really happened, especially since none of the gospels was written until at least 35 years after Jesus' earthly ministry?" The same sort of question could be asked about any of the narrative material in the Bible, but for Christians, it is of particular interest when it comes to the record of Jesus, the reason for and focus of our faith.

Remember that the gospels are not, and do not claim to be, historical records. They are theological reflections on the life, death, and resurrection of Christ. They represent how the earliest generation of Christians interpreted the church's memory of Jesus. The process of interpretation that led to the writing of the gospels is what provides us a true witness of how Jesus is our Savior.

Not long ago, I gained a new appreciation for how this process must have worked in the early church. While on a pastoral sabbatical in 2008, I journeyed to the Holy Land. My three-week excursion included a week by myself in Galilee, a week of hiking all over Israel with nine other pilgrims, and a week on my own in Jerusalem. I took copious notes on my experiences. I recorded every thought, every new insight, and every tidbit of new knowledge. I anticipated that during this once-in-a-lifetime pilgrimage, God would share a new, exciting word with me that would bring clarity and freshness to my ministry back home. And yet, except for one powerful experience of prayer near the beginning of my sojourn, I received no epiphany. On the last day of the trip, after I had packed my bags and was too exhausted to walk any more through the streets of the Old City, I recorded in my journal my disappointment that I had no more clarity about my ministry than the day I had arrived in Israel.

Soon after my return, I began organizing photos from my trip and creating a presentation to share with my church. I spoke about my Holy Land experience to my congregation over four consecutive Sunday nights. Then I began receiving invitations to make the same presentation in different formats—for a retreat at another church, for an evening lecture at a center for spiritual direction, and at a senior citizens apartment complex. I also began working pieces of the presentation into the New Testament courses I teach at a local college and through our conference's lay ministry training program. My sermon preparation over the next year kept bringing me back to places I had visited, ground I had traversed, and experiences I had soaked up. A year after my Holy Land journey, I wrote in my journal that, though I left Israel with no clear word from God, the truth of my pilgrimage had become apparent in my prayerful remembrance of it. It was only *as I interpreted it* that I came to see how God had indeed spoken powerfully to me in a way that had invigorated my ministry and changed my life.

In the same way, the New Testament reflects the interpretive memory of the early church. In those first days following Jesus' crucifixion, resurrection, and ascension into heaven, the disciples must have been in something of a daze, unable to make sense of all that had happened. They huddled in an upper room (perhaps the same one where Jesus had broken bread with them on the night of his betrayal), wondering what was next. But as they were pushed by the Holy Spirit into the world to share their experiences of Jesus' ministry and the risen Christ, they began to interpret what had happened and to put theological meat on the skeleton of events during their time with Jesus.

If the gospels gave us no more than an eyewitness news report of Jesus' life, death, and resurrection, we would only have a collection of facts. The narrative that gives meaning to our faith came through the memory and interpretation of early Christians. It is the memory of what happened that brings meaning to events—not the facts alone.

No evidence, no person, is ever remembered with pure objectivity. My maternal grandfather died when I was 16. His was the first significant loss in my young life. He was a self-made, hardworking farmer with strong calloused hands but a gentle touch for his grandchildren. My memory of him is important to me. I did not realize how great an impact he had made on me until after his death, when I began reflecting on how he spoke to me, how he included me in his farm work, and how proud he was of his extended family—especially at big holiday meals when he sat at the head of a long table in the old farmhouse. No one has the ability to reconstruct his life perfectly. Even if my family had the ability to do so, our memories would still interpret the facts we had. Those purely subjective memories do not obscure him; they enlarge his influence on us.

We will never be able to perfectly reconstruct the historical Jesus. And just as my siblings and I remember my grandfather in slightly different ways, so each of the four gospels presents us with a different way of remembering Jesus. It is Jesus *as remembered in Scripture* who calls us to commitment and service. This is the only Jesus the church, and indeed the world, has ever known. It is the belief of historic Christianity that *the interpretive memory of Jesus represented in the New Testament was guided by the Holy Spirit and thus presents us with a truthful representation of the Savior.* So while it is important to read the gospels with appreciation for the historical context both of Jesus' life and of the lives of the gospel writers, there is no need for us to seek a perfectly reconstructed Jesus of history. The *truth* of his life, death, and resurrection lies not in the facts of what happened, but in the Spirit-guided interpretive memory of his followers.

I do not mean to suggest that the gospels are divorced from history, or mere legend. Jewish and Roman historians attest to the existence of Jesus, who was also known as Messiah (or Christ). In addition, the gospels speak of individuals and groups of people who are also mentioned in ancient written sources other than the New Testament. They include the following:

John the Baptist. All four gospels record that John the Baptist baptized Jesus, and then soon after was arrested and killed by Herod Antipas, the Roman-appointed ruler over the region of Galilee. John was the leader of a movement that was highly critical of the temple leadership in Jerusalem. He warned that the kingdom of God was coming, and he preached the need for all people, even children of Abraham, to repent of their sins. John's preaching was "apocalyptic," meaning that he focused on the end of time and the coming judgment of God. (See the section on the Revelation.)

The gospels tell us that John spoke of the coming of one greater than himself. John baptized people in the Jordan River with water, but the one coming after him would "baptize ... with the Holy Spirit and fire" (Matthew 3:11). The way he is described in Matthew and Mark seems to link him to the Qumran community, a group of monastic Jews who were born into priestly families but rejected the corrupt temple priesthood. They withdrew from society and made their communal home in a network of caves overlooking the Dead Sea near the mouth of Jordan River. They spent their days in study, prayer, and the meticulous work of copying the words of the prophet Isaiah and writing their own view of the end of history. These writings, called the "Dead Sea Scrolls" when archeologists discovered them in 1947, are now on display at the Israel Museum in Jerusalem.

Pontius Pilate. Roman historical records confirm that Pontius Pilate served as the Roman procurator of Judea and sentenced Jesus to death for treasonous activity. The gospels present Pilate as an impatient and largely ineffective administrator who refused to take responsibility for the decision to have Jesus crucified, though it could happen only at his command. The Jewish philosopher Philo described him as "inflexible, stubborn, and cruel," while the Jewish historian Josephus blamed him for inciting numerous riots because of his insensitivity to Jewish culture.

The Sadducees. These are the wealthy elite of the city of Jerusalem who provided Judea with its temple priesthood. We can verify from records outside the Bible that the

Sadducees were the only Jews in Judea who enjoyed any political power, and that they cooperated with the Roman occupation of their land. For this, they were despised by most of the Jewish people. Sometimes, the gospels use the word "Sadducees," and other times the phrase "chief priests" or "chief priests and scribes" to describe them. While not all Sadducees were priests or scribes, the entire temple leadership came from this upper-class sect.

The Pharisees. We also know from sources other than the Bible that the principal opponents of the Sadducees were the Pharisees, whose name means "set apart." The Pharisees, whose teaching form the basis of the rabbinic Judaism that has survived to this day, sought to reform the practice of their faith by moving attention away from the temple toward smaller gathering places (*synagogues*) where rabbis (teachers) read the scriptures and explained their meaning to the people. Synagogues were set up all over Judea, so the Pharisaic movement spread across the land. Capernaum, the city where Jesus lived while he was ministering in Galilee, was a major center of the Pharisaic movement.

The gospels portray Jesus as very critical of the Pharisees, leading many readers of the New Testament to conclude that the Pharisees were his principal enemies who actively sought his death. In fact, there were Pharisees among Jesus' original followers, and scholars have been able to show that many of Jesus' teachings were similar or identical to that of the Pharisees. The disputes between Jesus and the rabbis of the time seem to stem from disagreements over the application of their teachings rather than fundamental differences of theology. In fact, Jesus says in Matthew 23:3, at the beginning of his strongest condemnation of the Pharisees, that his own followers should "do whatever they teach you and follow it; but do not do as they do." He goes on to accuse them of rampant hypocrisy because they required far more of their followers than of themselves.

The Zealots. For much of the first Christian century, a group of guerrilla fighters called "Zealots" were moving stealthily in the countryside and urban areas of Judea, looking for opportunities to gather a fighting force that could march against the Roman presence in Judea and win independence—the same way the Maccabees had driven the Greeks out of Jerusalem some 200 years earlier. (See the section on the Apocrypha.) The Zealots were known for having started a failed revolt in the year A.D. 6, and also for inciting the war with the Romans that began in A.D. 66 and led to the destruction of the temple in 70.

At least one, and probably two, of Jesus followers were Zealots. One of these, Simon, is identified as a Zealot in Luke 6:15. The other, Judas, is often presumed to be a Zealot who was waiting for Jesus to lead a revolt—and became disillusioned with him for refusing to accept any political or military power. Judas' betrayal of Jesus might have been committed out of disappointment and anger, or in an attempt to goad Jesus into defending himself in hopes of touching off a military revolt.

Herod the Great. According to Matthew and Luke, Jesus was born "in the days of King Herod of Judea" (Luke 1:5; see Matthew 2:1). Herod the Great is known from other sources to have been a masterful, sometimes ruthless, and often paranoid ruler. Appointed by Caesar Augustus in 37 B.C., he occupied the throne for more than three decades. He oversaw the construction of roads, aqueducts, and most famously, an ostentatious renovation of the Jerusalem temple. Herod's temple attracted Jewish and non-Jewish pilgrims from all over the world and greatly strengthened the Judean economy.

Matthew 2:16-18 says that Herod ordered the slaughter of all male infants two years and younger in Bethlehem in hopes of killing the infant Jesus. There is no other historical record of this event. However, such a decree is consistent with what we know of Herod's disposition near the end of his life, when a terrible disease aggravated his natural paranoia and kept him in constant agony.

Herod Antipas. When Herod the Great died, his kingdom was divided into three parts and bequeathed to three sons—Archeleus, Antipas, and Philip. Antipas ruled over the region of Galilee and built the city of Tiberius, named for the Roman Emperor under whom he served, on the Sea of Galilee (which became known as the Sea of Tiberias). In Matthew, Mark, and Luke, Herod Antipas (also called simply "Herod") orders the beheading of John the Baptist. In the gospel of Luke, Pontius Pilate sends Jesus to Antipas (who was visiting Jerusalem) for trial, arguing that a Galilean should be tried by the ruler of Galilee.

Caiaphas. Ancient Jewish records name Caiaphas as the high priest of Judaism who presided over the Sanhedrin (a Jewish law court also confirmed by historical sources) at the time of Christ. He is specifically mentioned in Matthew 26:57 and John 18:13 as questioning Jesus.

The remains of the house of Peter in Capernaum. Many archeologists believe this to be an authentic site. The innermost wall is of a first-century house. It contains markings of pilgrims from early Christianity designating it as the room where Jesus healed Peter's mother-in-law (Mark 1:30-31). Around this inner wall are the remains of a fourth-century church built over the site. The outermost wall is what is left of a twelfth-century church built on the ruins of the older church. The entire site sits underneath the modern St. Peter's church, whose sanctuary features a glass floor looking directly into the room of Peter's house.

In addition to these and other people who appear in the gospels, the geography of the Holy Land lends a texture of reality to the stories of Jesus. Jerusalem, Bethlehem, Capernaum, Nazareth, Bethsaida, Jericho, Caesarea Philippi, and other locations important to the gospel stories are real places, uncovered and preserved by archeologists, if not vibrant cities still today. The Judean Desert, the Jordan River, the rolling hills of Galilee, and the mountains of the north continue to call pilgrims across the ages back to the pages of the gospels.

Reading Paul

Essential Readings: Romans 3:21-6:23; 8:1-39; 12:1-21;
2 Corinthians 5:16-6:2; Galatians 3:6-29

The gospels, as central as they are, do not give us the entire picture of Jesus. It is also important to know some of the writings of Paul. For without Paul, Christianity probably would not have lasted longer than a century or two, and may never have emerged as a separate religion.

Some of the story of Paul can be found in the Acts of the Apostles. He is first mentioned in Acts 8:1 as approving of the stoning of Stephen, one of the early church's leaders. Acts 9:1-19 details the story of his conversion to Christ, and he emerges as the central figure of chapters 13-28. Paul also tells some of his own story in Galatians 1:13-2:14.

Paul was a contemporary of Jesus who was educated as a rabbi. He was zealous to define Jewish orthodoxy, and as a young man he sought to rid Judaism of all heresies, including the Christian movement. But during his days of persecuting the early church, he received a dramatic vision in which the risen Jesus confronted him personally. From that moment, Paul devoted himself to the cause of Christ as a missionary. When he first presented himself to the Christian church in Jerusalem, few trusted him, for they knew him as one of their persecutors, armed with the power of the temple authorities (Acts 9:26-30). He retreated to his home in Syria for an extended period. When he returned several years later, he received a warmer welcome. This time, he announced to the church that God had called him as an apostle to the Gentiles (non-Jews), and the church commissioned him for a missionary journey around the eastern side of the Roman empire.

Paul's ministry soon became controversial, for news reached Jerusalem that he had been baptizing Gentiles as followers of Jesus without requiring them to submit to Jewish laws. When Paul returned to Jerusalem, he explained his position to the church, saying that he believed Jesus Christ had torn down the barriers between Jews and Gentiles, so that Gentiles need not convert to Judaism to follow Christ (Acts 15:1-29). Though Paul was able to convince most of the Jerusalem Christians that he was right, a vocal minority protested and hounded him for the rest of his ministry, seeking to discredit him.

Nevertheless, Paul succeeded in beginning numerous churches around the empire and strengthening others that already existed. His stature was so great that churches recognized him as an apostle of Jesus, though he was not among the original twelve. The core of his beliefs, a theology that made Christianity a world religion, can be found in Romans 3 to 8 and Galatians 2 to 5. His letter to the Romans was written to the church in Rome at a time when Jewish-Christians were protesting the presence of so many Gentiles in their congregation. Paul founded the church in Galatia. But soon after he left them, they were visited by Paul's opponents, who intimidated these new Christians into being circumcised and submitting to the laws of Moses, saying Paul had misled them with a false gospel.

In these two writings, Paul says that God's covenant with Abraham was based entirely on faith. That is, the covenant did not depend on any ceremonial rite or adherence to a law code, but resulted purely from God's choice of Abraham, who "believed the Lord, and the Lord reckoned it to him as righteousness" (Genesis 15:6, quoted in Romans 4:3 and Galatians 3:6). Paul points out that the covenant, initiated in Genesis 12, preceded both circumcision (prescribed in Genesis 17) and the giving of the law (Exodus 20). Paul further says that anyone who believes that Jesus was raised from the dead is exhibiting the same kind of faith that Abraham showed and, by virtue of that faith, is included in the covenant. Jesus is therefore the Messiah, not just of the Jews, but of all people. In Christ, Paul says, all distinctions are eradicated. "There is no longer Jew or Greek, slave or free, there is no longer male and female, for all of you are one in Christ Jesus" (Galatians 3:28). An introductory reading of the New Testament needs to include this basic theological argument made by Paul.

PAUL THE APOSTLE

1. Paul's Conversion—*Galatians 1:13-24; Acts 9:1-30*
2. "The Covenant of Faith"—*Romans 3:21-8:39; Galatians 3:6-5:6*
3. The Resurrection of Christ—*1 Corinthians 15*

In the epistles to the Christians in Rome and Galatia, Paul spells out his theology plainly. Paul did not write his letters, however, for the purpose of teaching theology. He wrote to specific churches to address specific problems. Sometimes, as in Rome, the problem was a theological disagreement. At other times, he addressed ethical concerns. In his letters to the Corinthians, Paul gives direction on such matters as the advisability of marriage, sexual morality, whether to bring lawsuits against fellow Christians, and whether to eat meat that has been sacrificed to pagan gods. He also gives plentiful instruction about conduct in worship—the theme of a large block of material extending from chapters 11 to 14 in 1 Corinthians.

Much of Paul's ethical teaching is difficult for the contemporary reader because we are not familiar with the social practices, customs, and culture of the places to which Paul was writing. For this reason, Paul's letters are best studied in a group that has access to scholarly research that explains the context. Unless we understand the cultural context of these teachings, we cannot fully appreciate the underlying principles that still apply to our own time. It is also important to remember that Christ stands at the center of Scripture, and his ministry and teaching guide us in determining the relative importance of all other biblical texts—including New Testament texts outside the four gospels. Some of Paul's teachings are clearly more central to our faith than others. His majestic confession of faith in Galatians 3:28 that we are one in Christ carries more weight than his command that "if a woman will not veil herself, then she should cut off her hair" (1 Corinthians 11:6—a command given out of concern that Christian women not be confused with prostitutes in Corinth, who uncovered their heads and wore their hair down in public).

One overarching theme in Paul's ethical writings helps us put many of them into context. Like other Christians of his time, Paul believed that Christ's return to end history and fulfill God's kingdom would happen very soon—and that nothing was more important for Christian churches than to spread the gospel message as far and fast as possible. This concern led Paul to counsel against making major life changes like getting married (1 Corinthians 7:25-31), and also against unnecessarily offending the cultural sensibilities of the people of that time (1 Corinthians 11:2-16; 14:33-36).

Paul acknowledged that Christ had freed women from a patriarchal culture, but was concerned that the aggressive exercise of this freedom would be so controversial that churches would lose the ability to win converts to the Christian movement. The same might be said of slaves demanding freedom. Paul clearly opposed slavery on the grounds that God sees all men and women as equals (see Galatians 3:28 and the entire letter to Philemon, a slave-owner). But he also knew that if Christians became social radicals, they would only marginalize themselves and invite persecution.

This principle of placing the spread of the gospel above the exercise of our freedom in Christ is perhaps best expressed in Galatians 5:13: "For you were called to freedom, brothers and sisters, only do not use your freedom as an opportunity for self-indulgence, but through love become slaves to one another."

Also important to Paul's teaching is his understanding of Christian communities, which he calls "bodies of Christ." Just as all the parts of the human body are organically related to one another, and cannot declare independence from each other, so Christians are organically connected to one another—and Christ is the head of the body of which we are all members (see 1 Corinthians 12:12-26). Within this body, we are to practice the love, humility, and hospitality that was first and best exemplified by Christ himself. In this way, the church bears witness to the world of what the kingdom of God looks like. Good examples of this community ethic are found in Romans 12:9-21 and 14:1-15:13.

Letters Written in Paul's Name

Of the thirteen letters that belong to the "Pauline corpus" (the epistles attributed to Paul), only seven are widely accepted as having been written by Paul himself. The other six are disputed by New Testament scholars for reasons I noted at the beginning of this chapter. Just as it is important to understand the context in which Paul was writing, it is also important to know the later context from which Paul's disciples wrote. The letters to the Colossians and the Ephesians, probably composed in the last quarter of the first century, reflect the need at that time to bring some level of organization to the Christian movement, which was in danger of splintering into different sects. For this reason, these letters speak of the whole church as one "body of Christ," rather than separate bodies in different locations. They also express a highly developed theology designed to bring consensus to all Christians.

At least two of the "pastoral epistles," 1 Timothy and Titus, take the same concern even further, stipulating clear requirements for people who hold various offices in the church. Some of these requirements will strike today's readers as highly discriminatory of women, and indeed they are, because when these letters were written (the early second century), Christians lived under constant threat of persecution. Sheer survival had displaced almost every other concern. We need to consider these teachings in light of Christ's example of elevating women to roles formerly limited to men. As we read them, we should also appreciate the real threat of Christianity's annihilation by popular prejudice and state-sponsored persecution. An honest discussion of these texts needs to address when and whether it is ever appropriate for Christians to tolerate cultural prejudices or to avoid being seen as too far outside the cultural mainstream. As the later New Testament writings demonstrate, these were not simple issues for early Christians, nor are they for contemporary Christians.

The General Epistles

Essential Readings: Hebrews 4:14-8:13; 11:1-12:2

Since Paul's influence over the New Testament is so pervasive, it is easy to dismiss the epistles that have no connection to Paul. In truth, these other epistles have exercised less influence over the development of Christian belief. On the other hand, they continue to be Holy Scripture, so God speaks to us through them as well.

The longest extended theological argument about the nature of Christ in the New Testament is found in the letter (or sermon) to the *Hebrews*. (While the theology in Hebrews is not given as much attention as Paul's writings, it is still very important to the development of traditional Christian theology. For this reason, I have included portions of Hebrews in the list of "essential readings.") Neither the author nor the original audience of this epistle is known, though scholars have debated both for many centuries. The traditional view, suggested by the book's title, is that it was written to Jewish Christians living in Palestine around the time of the destruction of the Jerusalem temple in A.D. 70. If the tradition is correct, the letter's recipients had probably made up the Christian church in Jerusalem and then fled the city when war broke out with the Romans.

The writer of Hebrews seeks to assure his fellow believers that they have not abandoned their Jewish tradition, because Jesus is the fulfillment of that tradition. With the endangered (if not already destroyed) temple in mind, the writer speaks of Jesus as the perfect high priest who has made the perfect sacrifice—himself. This self-sacrifice makes atonement for the people and never needs to be repeated. Not only that, but the temple Jesus enters is heaven itself, not a building made with human hands. So his atoning sacrifice is good for all creation, not just the Jewish people. In this way, the writer of Hebrews comes to the same conclusion as Paul—that Christ's death was effective for the whole world—but he does so through a different image, focusing on Jesus as the perfect high priest in the true temple.

One key to understanding Hebrews is "the order of Melchizedek," a movement within Judaism that lifted up Melchizedek, the king of Salem, who in Genesis 14:18 is called "priest of God Most High." Melchizedek (whose name means "king of righteousness") brought bread and wine to Abraham and blessed him. In return, Abraham gave him a tithe of all his wealth. This seems to be a peace agreement between two important people who believed they worshiped the same God.

But later interpreters of Genesis saw something far more significant. A priest who could bless Abraham, and receive a tithe from him, had to be a messenger from God—perhaps even divine. The Dead Sea Scrolls, writings of the Qumran community dating to the time of Christ (see the section on John the Baptist), speak of Melchizedek as an angelic priest who will make atonement for the people when God fulfills the kingdom after the final judgment. The writer of Hebrews accepts this tradition and argues that Jesus is a priest "after the order of Melchizedek," who is "without father, without mother, without genealogy, having neither beginning of days nor end of life, but resembling the Son of God, he remains a priest forever" (Hebrews 7:3). He further argues that Melchizedek is only a forerunner of Christ, who did what Melchizedek could not do.

As both a human being and the Son of God, Jesus was made perfect through his sufferings, and his self-sacrifice was absolutely unique. Some of the most moving texts in this letter remind us that, because of his humanity, Jesus knows intimately all the struggles we face, and pioneers a trail of faith for us to follow. (See Hebrews 2:14-18; 4:14-16; and 12:1-2.) Most Christians today do not spend much time pondering the nature of Melchizedek, but the book of Hebrews provides insight into how early Jewish followers of Jesus, who were already critical of the temple priesthood, saw in Jesus a "better covenant" (Hebrews 8:6), a more promising way to uphold God's covenant with Israel than the politically charged temple-based Judaism of the time.

The letter of *James* was likely written to the same Jewish-Christian community that received Hebrews, but this shorter letter focuses entirely on ethical behavior in the community rather than theological belief.

1 and 2 Peter give counsel to Christians who are suffering persecution. They contain material that can easily be misused. Like the Pastoral Epistles, these letters need to be read as counsel in the midst of persecution. The "suffering" of women and slaves that seems to be endorsed in 1 Peter is not a maxim for Christian community, but encouragement for Christians who are being abused or persecuted by non-Christian husbands and slave-owners.

On the other hand, 1 Peter evidences a strong connection between early Christians and the Old Testament.

For instance, 1 Peter 2:9 calls the Christian community "a chosen race, a royal priesthood, a holy nation, God's own people," language reminiscent of the Torah's description of the nation Israel. (See Exodus 19:6 as an example.)

1, 2, and 3 John paint a sobering picture of one Christian community that split over a basic disagreement about the nature of Christ. The original community held to the belief that Jesus was fully human and also divine. The schismatic group that formed its own church believed that Jesus was not really human at all, but only appeared that way so humans could understand him. These letters remind us that, even in those early years, Christian communities could be highly conflicted, and sometimes split over doctrinal differences.

The tiny letter of *Jude* was probably composed sometime in the early second century to warn a Christian community about false teachings that could tear them apart. The writer speaks of "the faith that was once for all entrusted to the saints" (Jude 3), reminding us that one important function of churches in every generation is to faithfully maintain the tradition so it is not forgotten or corrupted by changing circumstances. As we have already seen, specific ethical practices and even theological images may change over time and in differing cultures, but certain basic principles—as well as faithful witness to the life, death, and resurrection of Christ—remain non-negotiable for Christians. Separating what is central from what is peripheral is the task of believers in every age, and always a matter of prayer, study, and careful discernment.

Reading the Revelation (or not!)

Some Christian traditions maintain that a basic reading of the Bible must also include apocalyptic literature. In fact, many fundamentalist groups consider the book of Revelation central to any study of the Bible. (This is because most Christian fundamentalists are also "dispensationalists." If you would like to know more about dispensationalism, refer to the note at the end of this section.)

Historically, the Christian church has not viewed apocalyptic literature in the Bible as centrally important. In fact, the Revelation almost failed to be included in the Bible. The book of Revelation was disputed as Scripture until the late fourth century. Even after it was included, many scholars challenged its status as Holy Scripture. Reformer Martin Luther, in his 1522 introduction to the Revelation, doubted the book's authority, maintaining that "Christ is neither taught nor known in it." He concluded that it is "neither apostolic nor prophetic."

Nevertheless, the Revelation is part of our Bible, and pieces of other biblical books, like Daniel, Zechariah, Isaiah, and Ezekiel are also apocalyptic—as is one major section from Jesus' teaching, found in Mark 13, Matthew 24, and Luke 21. We shouldn't attach more importance to this material than is warranted. Apocalypticism is *not* central to the Bible. Your salvation does not depend on being able to understand it. You can receive the gospel without ever cracking the book of Revelation. But apocalyptic is important, because through it, God does speak to us. It is God's word, like the rest of Scripture.

If you choose to venture into apocalyptic, be sure you have a basic understanding of the whole Bible first. Revelation is a terrible place to begin studying the Bible (which is why the early church put it at the end). Christian writer Eugene Peterson, in a commentary on Revelation entitled *Reversed Thunder,* wrote, "No one has any business reading the last book who has not already read the previous 65." While that standard may be unrealistic, the principle is correct. Revelation cannot be properly understood except within the context of all the Scripture.

HISTORICAL CONTEXT OF THE REVELATION

When reading apocalyptic, remember that it was written specifically for *persecuted* Christians. If you want to get into the apocalyptic mindset, imagine that a foreign power takes over the United States and demands that all citizens pay homage to a new leader by worshiping him as a god. You as a Christian refuse to do so. Because you pay no tribute at the official government altars honoring the leader, you are arrested, thrown into prison, and threatened with your life if you do not renounce your Christianity. You are banished to an isolation unit to think about your options. Meanwhile, members of your family are frightened for your safety and terrified that they, too, might be arrested.

Christians faced exactly that situation in the Roman empire. In the year 95, the emperor Domitian declared himself to be a god and demanded that all subjects of the empire worship him. The Christians refused, and Domitian ordered their arrest and execution. It was during this time that Revelation was written. In 167 B.C., Jews faced a similar crisis when the Greek emperor Antiochus IV declared his divinity and outlawed the practice of Judaism. During that time, the apocalyptic book of Daniel was written. All apocalyptic literature was written to encourage victims of religious persecution not to give up their faith or be afraid to die for what they believed in, because one day, God would avenge the blood of martyrs by destroying the power of their persecutors. One day, God would banish all evil from creation and establish a new kingdom of peace and justice that would include all God's faithful. Those who had died would be resurrected so they could enjoy God's new kingdom.

So the basic message of apocalyptic literature is really straightforward: those who endure through persecution will be glorified by God for their faithfulness, while those who have persecuted God's people will suffer the wrath of God's judgment. This message always carries incendiary political overtones. For instance, the Revelation condemns the Roman empire as an agent of the devil that will one day be abolished in favor of a "New Jerusalem."

But rather than condemning Rome openly, the book calls Rome "Babylon" and describes Rome as a whore riding a beast, "drunk with the blood of the saints" (17:5-6). This kind of symbolism serves two purposes. First, it masks the message of the book from those who don't know the "code," particularly the Roman persecutors. Second, those who do know the code are able to understand that what is happening to them has happened before to others. To call Rome "Babylon" is to compare the persecution of Christians with the persecution of Jews in an earlier time. The suffering of God's people is a fact of life in this world, not evidence that God has abandoned God's people.

THE USE OF SYMBOLISM

Apocalyptic writers made use of many different kinds of symbolism. The wild imagery unleashes creative imagination and gives hope to those being persecuted. The most important source of symbolism in Revelation is the Hebrew Scriptures, with which Revelation's first readers were very familiar. In its 404 verses, there are 350 references to the Old Testament. Therefore, familiarity with the Old Testament is helpful in understanding this book.

Numerology was also important in all apocalyptic literature. In the ancient Middle East, numbers were less significant for their mathematical function than for what they symbolized. A fairly uniform numerology developed among Semitic cultures that is evident in biblical apocalyptic and is outlined below.

Three symbolizes divinity. This is probably because in many pagan religions, there were three important gods: a male creator god, a female god of fertility, and an evil god of destruction. It is interesting that in Christianity, we understand God as Trinity, so the number three is also an appropriate Christian symbol for God.

Four is the number of the earth, since there are four seasons, four basic elements (earth, wind, fire, and water, according to ancient belief), and because people believed the earth was flat and had four corners.

Five and *ten* symbolize humanity, since human beings have ten fingers and ten toes, five on each hand and foot.

Seven symbolizes perfection or completion, since it is the sum of four (earthly completion) and three (God).

Three and a half, half of seven, symbolizes incompleteness. For instance, a period of 3½ years means a "limited period of time."

Six, one less than seven, represents imperfection.

Twelve is the product of four and three and represents organized religion, or the people of God. There were twelve tribes of Israel in the Old Testament and twelve apostles in the New Testament.

These numbers can be combined for symbolic purposes as well. For instance, three groups of seven clearly refer to God. The book of Revelation revolves around the breaking of seven seals, the blowing of seven trumpets, and the pouring out of seven bowls of incense. This can only mean that what is happening is the work of God. Three sixes, on the other hand, like the number 666, is imperfection pretending to be God, which is diabolical. Also, 12 times 12 is 144, which represents the people of God of both the Old and New Testaments. The number 144,000 is symbolic of all God's people through all time.

Other sources of symbolism for apocalyptic writers were colors and animals. The use of these symbols is less uniform across the spectrum of apocalyptic but not difficult to understand. For instance, white commonly represents purity, and a lion usually represents strength. In reading apocalyptic, it is important to remember that when colors and animals are used, they are nearly always symbolic of something else.

Unfortunately, many popular interpretations of apocalyptic seek to sensationalize its contents as representing current events that portend the end of the world. A serious study of apocalyptic, however, will take into account the historical context in which it was written. To glean God's word through this material, we need to appreciate what God was saying to its first readers—and then ask how that message applies to us.

THE APOCALYPTIC MESSAGE

The message of apocalyptic material in the Bible almost always comes down to these basic principles:

1. Whenever human governments and economic systems are invested with too much power, they become corrupt and perpetuate evil. Christians must never place our ultimate faith in human institutions of any kind. They can never substitute for the sovereignty of God.
2. When God's people suffer persecution, it is not because God is punishing them. It is because other powerful forces are at work in the world to destroy God's kingdom. God is always present with the persecuted, giving them strength to endure.
3. One day, God will bring a decisive end to the power of evil and establish justice throughout creation. Just as God had the first word in creation, God will also have the final word. No matter how much injustice the world endures, God will accomplish God's

purposes in the end. Nothing on earth or in heaven is more powerful than God.

4. The purpose of God's final judgment is not destruction but redemption. One of the most common misunderstandings of the Revelation is that God is going to destroy the earth with fire. But actually, it teaches that God will redeem both heaven and earth and remove the chasm between them.

The Revelation affirms these principles, but also goes further, assuring us that Christ, "the Lamb that was slaughtered" (Revelation 5:12), stands with his followers in the midst of every challenge, hardship, and persecution. Christ is worthy to be praised in persecution and in peace, on earth and in heaven, now and forever. It is fitting that even after the word "Amen," the Revelation repeats the plea of all Christians in every age: "Come, Lord Jesus." First and foremost, this book reveals Christ.

NOTE ON DISPENSATIONALISM

Dispensationalists believe that human history is divided into several broad epochs, called "dispensations," which are distinguished by how God relates to human beings within each one. Most dispensationalists believe that history is divided into seven dispensations. In each, God establishes a new covenant that changes the rules for how people attain salvation. For instance, the first dispensation began in the Garden of Eden. God gave Adam and Eve certain rules to live by. Those rules defined how God related to human beings until the time of the flood, when God spared Noah and established with him a new covenant, which became the new basis for God's relationship to humanity. The next dispensation commenced when God made a covenant with Abraham, the fourth when God gave the Ten Commandments, and so on.

From this point of view, we are now in the final dispensation, nearing the time when Jesus will return to earth in bodily form, take all true Christians immediately to heaven (an event referred to as "the rapture"), and carry out God's final judgment. Because we are so near the end times, say dispensationalists, those parts of Scripture that relate to the end of history have now been illuminated. In other words, the true meaning of the book of Revelation has remained a mystery until the dawning of the last dispensation. And now this book, as well as other apocalyptic material (usually referred to as "prophecy" by dispensationalists) is the new basis upon which God relates to human beings. Therefore this material is the most important in the Bible for us to understand.

Dispensationalism is a relatively new phenomenon. It dates to the 1700s among Scottish Protestants. It was popularized in the United States during periods of religious revival, and became mainstream among conservative Protestants in the twentieth century. Still, it does not represent classical Christianity. To be fair, Christianity has always been dispensationalist to a point. Christians believe that when God became flesh in Jesus Christ, something new happened that altered the universe. So from our perspective, there are two "dispensations" in human history: before Christ and after Christ. (Our calendars reflect this belief. We count time as either B.C.—before Christ—or A.D.—for the Latin *Anno Domini*, "in the year of our Lord." Some scholars, wishing to avoid the Christian connotation, substitute the abbreviations B.C.E.—before the common era—and C.E.—common era.) Any further divisions of history take attention away from the centrality of Christ's life, death, and resurrection.

CHAPTER 4

INTERPRETING
THE BIBLE

ONCE YOU HAVE read enough of the Bible to gain a broad understanding of its contents, you will want to explore it more deeply. You will have a whole new set of questions to guide your search. Many of your questions will likely concern interpretation. Once you accept that the Bible is the Word of God, you must ask *how* it is the Word of God. How much control did God exercise over the writers of Scripture? How does God speak to us through the Bible? How much of it should we take literally? Which texts are most important—and do certain texts take on more significance in certain situations or cultural contexts? What is the best way to apply the Bible to your life, your family's life, and how you interact with your community? Your own style of interpretation will take years to develop. You should not feel pressured to settle these issues all at once. But it is important to be aware of how you are reading the text as part of your own spiritual growth.

The Debate about Interpretation

Today in American Christianity, questions about the interpretation of Scripture are hotly debated. This is largely due to the rapid growth of fundamentalism during the last century. Fundamentalists are "inerrantists," which means they believe that every word in the Bible appears exactly as God personally directed the authors to write it. That is, authors were miraculously given exact details in areas of knowledge they could not have otherwise known. According to this view, the Bible cannot contain any errors of any kind (hence the name "inerrantist"). It must always be interpreted literally, except where literalism is clearly not intended (as in the poetic material or in the case of Jesus' metaphorical statements like "I am the gate" and "I am the true vine").

Many faithful Christians find this view impossible to hold. A literal reading of Scripture excludes the possibility of evolution, not to mention a universe where the earth orbits the sun, and the earth is round instead of flat. There is no getting around the fact that the writers of the Bible held assumptions about the physical universe that we now know are wrong. They also wrote from the perspective of a deeply patriarchal culture that subjugated women and condoned slavery. From an inerrantist position, God would not have allowed the biblical writers to write from an erroneous scientific or social perspective. Therefore, whatever they wrote about the physical universe or human relationships had to be correct.

Unfortunately, many people react to fundamentalism by dismissing the Bible as an antiquated book full of errors.

Within some liberal sectors of Christianity, the authority of the Bible is dismissed because of the faulty cultural assumptions held by its writers. Other Christians maintain that the Bible is not God's word, but only *contains* God's word, which must be carefully separated from the erroneous words of human beings also found there. This position puts the reader in the untenable position of having to judge which parts of Scripture are God-inspired and which are not.

There is an alternative to inerrancy that does not compromise the authority of the Bible as God's Word. Many conservative and centrist Christian scholars insist that both divine and human elements are involved in the writing of Scripture. All Scripture is inspired by God (the claim Scripture makes for itself in 2 Timothy 3:16), even though much of it reflects the style, personality, and cultural context of its authors. God did not tamper with the authors' humanity, but neither did God allow the authors' limited perspective to prevent God from speaking through the words they wrote. This means we are not at liberty to choose which parts of the Bible we will hold up as Scripture. Rather, we must wrestle with all of it, always asking what God is saying to us through the text—even those portions that make us uncomfortable or offend our sensibilities. According to this view, *the Bible is true in every matter it addresses to the degree of precision intended by God and possible for the writer.*

To say the entire Bible is inspired by God does not mean every word is equally important. When I was young, my parents taught me many things that were true, but not all those lessons were of equal importance. I needed to know

I should look both ways before crossing the street, but that was not nearly as important as knowing my parents loved me. Similarly, Paul's admonition to "take a little wine for the sake of your stomach" (1 Timothy 5:23) does not carry as much weight as John 3:16: "For God so loved the world that he gave his only Son." Some parts of Scripture are clearly more important than others. Still, God's Word is present throughout.

Judging the relative importance of Scripture may seem just as problematic as sorting out God's Word from the words of humanity, but we have help. The gospels are the central focus of all Scripture for Christians, for Christ is the Word made flesh (John 1:14). Christ himself said of his critics, "You search the scriptures because you think that in them you have eternal life; and it is they that testify on my behalf" (John 5:39). We do well to remember these words. The Bible does not save us, but points toward the one who saves. Therefore, we should always interpret the Bible in light of the teachings of Christ. Learning how to do this will take time, and it is not a clear-cut process. But as we pray, worship, and fellowship with other Christians, we invite Christ to dwell within us. The more we open our lives to the presence of Christ, the more insight we will gain into the truth of Scripture.

This does not mean, however, that piety is a substitute for rigorous study. If Christ dwells in us, he will also dwell in our minds. As contemporary readers of the Bible, we need to use whatever tools are available to understand the context of the writing and separate the cultural and personal biases of the writers from the eternal truths they seek to communicate. Just as the Bible has been translated from Hebrew and Greek into our own language, so we must translate its message from the context of the ancient world to our own context to understand what God is saying to us.

For some Christians, this raises a question. Why doesn't God speak to us plainly? Why do we have to be concerned with translations, history, culture, and interpretation to understand God's Word in the Bible? Couldn't God have made it easier?

No doubt, God could have dropped from heaven a Bible saying exactly what God wanted it to say. But who could understand it? What language would it be written in? If it were given directly by God, *it wouldn't be in human language, and we couldn't understand it.* That's why the Bible didn't fall out of the sky, but was prompted by God's Spirit through the real lives of real human beings. The biblical writers were not robots. They were flesh and blood people, dealing with the same fears, hopes, anxieties, and joys any of us experience. If they had been suddenly lifted out of their own context, they wouldn't be human anymore, and nothing they said would make any sense to other human beings. Just as God dwelled among us through a human being named Jesus, so God's Word has come to us through the words, experiences, and cultural contexts of human beings.

Therefore, responsible Bible study involves study of the history and culture of the biblical era. As readers, we seek to place ourselves as much as possible in the cultural context of the Bible so we can understand the eternal principles being applied in that context. It is in those underlying principles—not just their application to a particular context—that God speaks to us. So we must not remain in the world of the biblical writers. The task of interpreting Scripture is not complete until we return to our own context and apply biblical principles to our own lives. This is not easy. It requires a rigorous commitment that takes years to develop, but it is also a deeply rewarding journey of faith.

Reading the Bible on Multiple Levels

Inerrantists often insist their view of Scripture is simply the traditional view of Christians. But in fact, inerrancy is a modern understanding that seeks to make the Bible conform to a modern, scientific understanding of truth. Fundamentalists believe that if a statement is not factually true, then it isn't true at all. Modern science, with its emphasis on "verifiability," has led our culture to insist that unless something is factually true, then it must be false.

We must not impose this standard on the Bible. Historically, religion has not equated truth with fact. Jesus certainly did not believe that truth had to be factual. Many of his teachings were in the form of fictional stories called "parables." No one would argue that these stories told by Jesus are not "truthful."

The Scriptures communicate truth in many different ways. For this reason, Christian scholars since the earliest days of the church have maintained that the Bible can be read and interpreted on many different levels. If we stop with only a literal reading, we cannot hope to confront the fullness of God's Word. If Bible study is going to help us grow in our relationship to God, we must be willing to move beyond a surface reading of the text.

Whenever you read the Bible, the most important question is, "What is God saying through this text?" After all, if the Bible is God's Word, then its primary purpose is to serve as a means by which God speaks to us. Staying focused on this primary question will help you move beyond a literal reading of the text. Even those biblical texts that *should* be taken literally need to be explored below the surface to find their deeper meaning.

JESUS WALKING ON WATER

John 6:15-21 tells the story of Jesus walking on water. What is God telling us in this account? You could say that God is telling us Jesus *really did* walk on water. But what difference would that make? How does that deepen your relationship to God? When you read the story more closely, you will see it can be interpreted on a spiritual level. Jesus walked on water through a storm, and he calmed the storm to prevent the disciples' boat from capsizing. The story teaches that Jesus is with us when life's storms get rough. The text also says the disciples were afraid when they first saw Jesus, but then Jesus spoke to them and said, "Do not be afraid." Is the story also about our own fears—not only of the storms, but also of Jesus' presence with us in the storms? Are we afraid of having faith?

As probing as such questions are, we cannot stop with them. The story concerns even more. As he approaches the disciples' boat, Jesus says, "It is I." Translated literally from the Greek, he said, "I am," which is how God identified himself to Moses in the burning bush (Exodus 3:14). Now we see that this text also serves an important theological purpose. Jesus identifies himself as one and the same with the God of the exodus; the great "I Am" of the Hebrew Scriptures. Jesus was not merely a prophet of God; he was God in the flesh. The divinity of Jesus is one of the most important themes of the gospel of John.

We have now looked at the story of Jesus walking on water on three levels: literal, spiritual, and theological. If the only question you ask of the text is "Did Jesus really walk on water?" you have not scratched the surface of its meaning.

In fact, by the time you get to the theological level of the story, the question of its factual accuracy has become much less important. Many Christians choose to believe that Jesus literally walked on water. But if that's all they learn from this story, they might as well not believe it even on a literal level. Other Christians believe this story is more legend than fact. If they conclude on that basis that the story is "untruthful," they have not confronted at all the meaning of the text.

People from both groups can study the text and agree that God is telling them to take heart in the midst of life's storms, and not to be afraid of meeting God in those storms. The crucial issue is whether we have received God's word from the story and whether we allow God's word to make a difference in how we live.

Giving Away Your Wealth

Another text we need to read on more than one level is Matthew 19:16-22. In this story, a man came to Jesus and asked how to receive eternal life. Jesus told him to obey the commandments, and he listed some of them. The man replied that he had obeyed all those and asked, "What do I still lack?" Jesus told him to sell his possessions, give the money to the poor, and follow him. But the man went away sorrowful, "for he had many possessions."

A simple, literal reading of this story (and the parallel accounts in Mark 10 and Luke 18) suggests that to follow Jesus, you must become destitute. If that were true, then the vast majority of Christians in every age of the church have placed themselves in great spiritual peril. Clearly, very few Christians believe they should take this story literally. In fact, because this text makes many of us so uncomfortable, we relativize its meaning: "Jesus wanted *him* to give away all his money, but that is not what Jesus wants *me* to do. This story doesn't really apply to me." But *something* about this story must apply to all of us, or it wouldn't be Scripture. So we must probe more deeply.

If you are familiar with the Ten Commandments, you might notice that in this story Jesus lists only six, and all six have to do with how we relate to other people. You will also notice that the four Jesus omitted all have to do with worshiping God. So when the man asks, "What do I still lack?" the implicit answer is "obedience to the first four commandments." This suggests that Jesus' instruction for the man to divest himself of his material wealth was a concrete way to fulfill the first four commandments. He needed to be free of his material possessions because his wealth had become his god. He could not worship God and continue to cling to his possessions in an idolatrous way.

Now the Bible confronts us with all sorts of questions regarding our own lives. Are we guilty of idolatry? Are there any things in our lives that are more important to us than God? Would we be willing to give those up to have eternal life? Jesus, at the very least, is saying there is no price too high to be free of idolatry. Do we believe that? And let's not shy away from the issue of material possessions. Isn't it true that wealth often *does* become idolatrous? In verse 24, Jesus tells his disciples, "It is easier for a camel to go through the eye of a needle than for someone who is rich to enter the kingdom of God." How confident can we really be that we are not just as shackled to our possessions?

There is an even deeper level of this story, too. It has to do with the notion of "goodness." In the account of this episode in Luke's gospel (Luke 18:18-29), the man addresses Jesus as "good teacher," and Jesus asks him why he used the term "good." The man says he has obeyed all the commandments Jesus lists. If he has, then he would be what society considers a "good" person. One has to wonder if the man expected Jesus to say, "You're a good person. You have nothing to worry about. Eternity is yours."

If this is a story about idolatry, then perhaps it is partly about idolizing "goodness"—seeking above all else to be known as a good person—as though the whole purpose of life is to be nice to others. When we pride ourselves on being good, our idea of God is reduced to a scorekeeper who keeps track of our ethical behavior. That is a safe God who will never ask us to take risks. You cannot truly worship God by just being good. Passages like this lead us to ask penetrating questions about ourselves and our behavior. We find that as we read them closely, they begin to read us as well.

PAUL'S TEACHING ON FAMILIES

This example deals with a very different kind of text. In Ephesians 5:21-6:8, Paul (or someone writing in his name) talks about family relationships. He says things that disturb our modern sensibilities: "Wives, be subject to your husbands ... slaves, obey your earthly masters." Taken out of context, these passages can be—and often are—used to support sexism and the idea that slavery (practiced with Christian compassion) is permissible. That is a very superficial reading of the text that doesn't do it justice.

In the first place, note that the opening statement to the whole passage reads, "Be subject to one another out of reverence for Christ." That is the topic sentence—the guiding principle—of the whole text. Yes, wives should submit to their husbands, but that submission is mutual. Husbands should also love their wives as Christ loved the church. To be sure, Paul's comparison of men to Christ and women to the church in verses 25-33 conveys his cultural patriarchal bias. But within that patriarchy, he puts forward an amazingly progressive view of marriage. He extends the same principle of mutual submission to the parent-child relationship ("Children, obey your parents ... Fathers, do not provoke your children to anger") and to the master-slave relationship ("Slaves, obey your earthly masters ... Render service with enthusiasm ... And, masters, do the same to them").

Further study of Paul's cultural context leads us to recognize that Paul is quoting the Roman law of *paterfamilias*, which established a clear hierarchy in the home. This law, regarded as the backbone of Roman civilization, granted civil status only to the "father of the family" and relegated every other member of the household—wife, children, and slaves—to the status of property. *Paterfamilias* was completely antithetical to Christian principles. But in this passage, Paul gives pastoral advice to Christians who must live with the law even though they don't agree with its principles. He provides a Christian commentary on *paterfamilias* that turns the Roman principle of submission into the Christian principle of mutual submission.

In the Christian household, women are not property; they are as precious to their husbands as the church is to Christ. Children are not objects of authoritarian rule, but the responsibility of their parents to raise up in the knowledge of the Lord. Slaves, in the eyes of God, are no different from their masters. In fact, if masters treat their slaves the same way slaves treat their masters, the institution of slavery is undone—not through revolution or legal means, but through submission to the true head of any household, Christ.

Paul's teaching, far from a defense of patriarchy, turns out to be a subtle, incendiary teaching that will transform society from the ground up. Paul has upheld two important principles. First, he endorses the Christian principle of mutual submission within the Christian household. Second, he discourages Christians from open revolt against an unjust Roman law. Instead, he counsels Christians to live faithfully in accordance with the ethics of Christ and to allow the gospel to transform society through their witness as an alternative community.

How do we apply these principals to our own context? Shouldn't we be as progressive (or radical) in our context as the Ephesian Christians were in theirs? What will that mean for our families? How do we embody this principal of mutual submission, and how do we witness against the unjust family relationships that exist in our communities?

A discussion of contemporary family life is not likely to address slavery, but it will probably address more than sexism. Is there injustice in how busy our families have become? Or in how materialistic? Are there other forms of family injustice that are perpetuated by the reigning culture? How can Christians resist them by making alternative life choices? Throughout this discussion, we must never lose sight of the primary question: *What is God saying* to today's families through this text written 2,000 years ago?

Text and Tradition

A very important reason to read the Bible for ourselves—and one purpose of biblical scholarship—is to sort out differences between what biblical texts actually say and how religious tradition remembers them. Sometimes tradition "fills in the blanks," providing details to Bible stories that leave much to the imagination. Other times, tradition interprets stories in ways that change their original meaning.

LIFE IN EDEN

Such is the case with the story of Adam and Eve in the garden of Eden, which Christian tradition remembers as "the fall of humanity." Idyllic life in Eden is destroyed because Eve yields to temptation when a talking serpent entices her to ignore God's prohibition and eat the forbidden fruit of the

Tree of Knowledge of Good and Evil. Commonly, the serpent is identified with the devil, and the violation of God's rule is interpreted as an irreversible descent (or fall) into sin that condemns the entire human race. God's expulsion of Adam and Eve from the garden is then seen as the loss of a perfect existence (inspiring John Milton's *Paradise Lost*), which in turn implies that our salvation amounts to a return to Eden. The term "paradise," which means "garden," is appropriate to describe Eden, but sometimes "paradise" is used interchangeably with "heaven," as when Jesus said to one being crucified with him, "Today you will be with me in Paradise" (Luke 23:43). Does the garden of Eden represent heaven? A common notion that has circulated for centuries in Christian circles is that before "the fall," Adam and Eve were immortal, and death was punishment for their sin, but Christ has erased that punishment by restoring to us eternal life—the immortality Adam and Eve were given originally.

While there can be no doubt that Genesis bears witness to a tragic rupture in God's relationship to humanity, many of the traditional assumptions about this story deserve close scrutiny. For instance, the word "fall" is not found in the story. Jewish scholars are quick to point this out and dismiss the idea of "the fall" as a Christian misreading of their Scripture. Also, nowhere is there any indication that the serpent is the devil. The only adjective used to describe the serpent is "crafty" (3:1). At no point is the serpent explicitly associated with evil. The story also makes plain that immortality was never God's intention for human beings, even in the garden of Eden. The "Tree of Life" (immortality) is hidden from Adam and Eve, and the reason

God gives for expelling them after they have eaten from the Tree of Knowledge of Good and Evil is that "he might reach out his hand and take also from the tree of life, and eat, and live forever" (3:22). Adam and Eve are thrown out of Eden to *prevent* human immortality. Christians share the hope of eternal life through resurrection, meaning that God raises us from death to *new* life. Had Adam and Eve been immortal, they would never have died. Life in their earthly bodies would have continued forever.

Finally, there is reason to question whether Eden is in fact the "perfect" existence. If that is true, then it follows that the entire biblical drama would be about returning humanity to that same paradise—reversing "the fall" by restoring the original habitat of the first humans. And yet the fulfillment of creation at the end of the Bible is not a garden but a city: "I saw the holy city, the New Jerusalem, coming down out of heaven from God" (Revelation 21:2). Rather than the simple innocence of Eden, a city implies a web of complex relationships that strive for peace and justice. This suggests that, even had there been no disobedience in the garden, God would not have been content with the human race remaining in blissful ignorance. Even an unbroken relationship of trust between God and humans would eventually have led to a "city" where human beings wrestle with the challenges of living in community and work together to achieve true harmony as the population becomes more and more diverse.

As we read the story of Adam and Eve and remove the cloak of tradition, we confront the story as it actually appears in the Scriptures. We find ourselves asking all sorts of interesting questions: Why did God forbid the fruit of the Tree of Knowledge of Good and Evil? Had Adam and Eve remained in Eden long enough, would God have invited them to eat of this fruit—or would they have always remained ignorant of the knowledge it provided? (One early Christian theologian suggested the sin of Adam and Eve should be understood as a "fall upwards," because eating the fruit freed them from the static existence of the garden and made possible humanity's quest for meaning and purpose.) Is Eden the "perfect" existence—the sort of place you would want to spend eternity? Or does it seem more like a beginning place for the relationship between God and humanity?

In Genesis 4:7, God tells Cain, "Sin is lurking at the door; its desire is for you, but you must master it." Where did sin originate? How does the story of Adam and Eve help us answer this?

It is no wonder that tradition has colored how we read the opening chapters of Genesis, because these ancient texts raise so many questions. While tradition may help us find the answers, we must never let traditional answers substitute for reading the text itself. Sometimes the Word of God comes to us in the form of a question rather than an answer!

THE BIRTH OF CHRIST

Another text that is remembered more through the lens of tradition than for what it actually says is the story of Jesus' birth in Luke 2:1-7. The popular image of Jesus' birth is a scene that includes the holy family, plenty of livestock, shepherds, three kings who have come to pay homage to Jesus, and angels singing above a barn-like stable bathed in heavenly light. This pastoral scene bears little resemblance to what the text describes.

Luke begins by telling us about a decree issued by the emperor in Rome that uprooted many families in Judea— including Joseph and Mary, who were forced to travel the rocky terrain from Nazareth to Bethlehem when Mary was nearly nine months pregnant. Luke does not dwell on any details other than "the time came for her to deliver her child" and "she gave birth to her firstborn son and wrapped him in bands of cloth, and laid him in a manger, because there was no place for them in the inn" (Luke 2:6-7). If we focus only on the details Luke provides, we are struck by the humble circumstances of the birth of the Messiah, precipitated by the oppressive politics of the Roman Empire.

While the next few verses relate the familiar story of the angels announcing the Messiah's birth to shepherds in a nearby field, we notice quickly that Luke does not mention anything about three kings visiting the Christ child. The second chapter of the gospel of Matthew does relate the story of "wise men (Magi) from the East" coming to see Jesus, but here again we are confronted with a story that tradition has to some extent rewritten. In Matthew's account, the visitors are not kings, and Matthew never says there were three of them, only that they brought three kinds of gifts. The focus is less on the circumstances of their visit than on the larger political realities into which Jesus was born: a political king, Herod, who is jealous and paranoid, seeks to have Jesus killed—even if it means killing every male infant in Bethlehem.

ABRAHAM'S NEAR SACRIFICE OF ISAAC

Popular tradition can get in the way of what Scripture actually says. But sometimes tradition helps us grapple with difficult texts. A good example is the story in Genesis 22:1-14, where God tells Abraham to sacrifice his son Isaac. If you have read the story of Abraham to that point, you know he had waited a very long time—far past the years of childbearing, for this son to be born. You also know that this son is the only hope for God to fulfill his promise to Abraham that he would be "the ancestor of a multitude of nations" (Genesis 17:5).

The demand to sacrifice Isaac, therefore, makes no sense and forces Abraham into a terrible dilemma. As you read the story, you are troubled not only by the illogic of the request. You might also be deeply offended that God would ask such a thing of any parent, even if God didn't intend to allow the sacrifice. You are relieved that, just before Abraham slays his son, an angel intervenes and provides a ram for the sacrifice. But that doesn't erase the agony that Abraham had endured. What kind of God would even suggest such a horrible act?

Tradition, both Christian and Jewish, has wrestled with this question. In the Middle Ages, the story was popularly seen as an allegory pointing toward the death of Jesus, God's only Son. A comparison was made between Abraham and God. The human father was allowed to spare his son, but the heavenly Father did not spare *his* only Son, proving how much God loved the world. This allegorical understanding invites reflection on the agony that God endured in giving up Jesus for our sake.

Another traditional interpretation, popular with the Protestant reformers in the sixteenth century, is that this story is entirely about faith. God was testing the strength of Abraham's faith, and God only needed to know that Abraham was willing to do the unthinkable in obedience to God. This interpretation invites us to consider the strength of our own faith—and whether we are willing to take great risks to follow God. It also challenges us to consider that sometimes what we are led to do in faith may not be the most logical or prudent course. This interpretation may also invite an honest discussion about the limits of our faith, and perhaps even raise questions about whether God's request of Isaac was ethical under any circumstances. Even questions that challenge God's motives are questions about our relationship to God and need to be stated honestly.

A third interpretation, from the Jewish tradition, has been noted by Christian scholars as well. Abraham was still getting to know God and was having to do so in a land where many other gods were worshiped. A common characteristic of other Middle Eastern religions was the sacrifice of first-born children. Perhaps Abraham dreaded, but expected, God to make this request. If so, God played to his expectations before stopping him at the last minute to show dramatically that God would never require human sacrifice. This interpretation shifts the focus to the value God places on every human life.

Of course, reading the Bible alone does not give us access to any of these traditions. We learn them through our connection to the Christian community—either through additional reading, regular worship, or Christian teaching. The value of reading Scripture is diminished when we read it in isolation from the faith communities for which it is written. The purpose of this book is to encourage people to overcome a sense of inadequacy or intimidation and read the Bible for themselves. On the other hand, Bible reading should never be a purely solitary activity. It is written for communities of people. We cannot truly live in relationship to God without pursuing healthy relationships with others who are also seeking to be in covenant with God.

Within the broader Christian community, the Bible is interpreted many ways. Any interpretive method has value if it takes the Bible seriously as God's Word. When theories of interpretation become more important than paying attention to what God is saying, they lose their value. As long as you stay focused on discerning God's Word in Scripture, and remain in dialogue with other people of faith who are also discerning God's Word, you will develop an interpretive style that fits your personality and allows God to speak to you.

Living with the Bible

If at this point you are still intrigued by the study of the Bible, it is time to move beyond this primer. Three principles are important to keep in mind.

First, join a group of people who are studying the Bible. Personal Bible reading is a good discipline, but it needs to be complemented by group study. The Bible tells us that God relates to us through communities of people, like Israel and the church. When we rely solely on our own wisdom to understand Scripture, we are likely to distort its meaning. The whole Bible is about covenants. It would make no sense, then, to try to interpret it without being part of some kind of a covenantal community. Churches need to provide group Bible studies that are led by people who are already familiar with the Bible and who are not afraid to let participants ask honest questions about the text.

Second, seek out the help of scholars. You cannot be expected to know about historical and cultural context without some serious study. Good scholars work to make their findings available to the whole church (not just fellow scholars!), so our study can be more fruitful. A good Bible study leader will be familiar with scholarly material and can discuss it with a group. Still, at some point you may want to read this material yourself. Look for biblical commentaries written specifically for lay people. One classic lay commentary was written over a half century ago, but it is still in print: William Barclay's *Daily Study Bible Series*. Professor Barclay wrote only about the New Testament, but other scholars have added to his work with commentaries on Old Testament books. When you have reached a level of study where you would like to use commentaries, ask your pastor or Bible study leader for suggestions.

Third, let the Bible set the agenda of your study. Often, people who don't know the Bible come to it in times of desperation, seeking quick answers that will solve personal problems. They want to know what the Bible says about divorce, sexuality, family, alcoholism, or whatever difficulty they are facing. The Bible is not an answer book. It is a book you have to live with. Extended study of the Scriptures over a long period will eventually help you discern how to handle any situation you must face. We cannot expect the Bible to offer quick answers to people who are not willing to make a commitment to hearing God's Word.

Studying the Bible is a form of listening to God. Therefore, it is a kind of prayer. It is one important way to grow in your relationship to God. Approached with humility, patience, and a willingness to learn, Bible study will change your life. You will gain tremendous knowledge—not just academic knowledge, but wisdom for how to live. You will grow in your understanding of yourself, of the human race, and of God. And you will never stop learning. Even the world's greatest scholars of the Bible will confess that, no matter how much time they spend in study, the Bible continues to speak to them in new ways.

When people discover the power of Bible study, they may be tempted to claim more for the Bible than it claims for itself. In fact, some forms of Christianity seem to *worship* the Bible, as if learning, memorizing, and quoting Scripture is all that is required of Christians. It is important to remember that the Bible is not God; it is a witness to God. So study of the Bible should lead beyond itself, whetting our appetites to explore other ways to strengthen our relationship to God through prayer, worship, and service. Those new experiences of our faith will in turn lead us back into the Scriptures to learn more than we were able to glean before.

The Bible is a wonderful gift, given to all people. It speaks to people who are just getting to know God, as well as to people of faith who want to know God more intimately. It is a precious vessel that holds the wisdom of people across thousands of years who have listened for God and heard God's voice. You are invited to join these saints and let God speak to you.

CPSIA information can be obtained
at www.ICGtesting.com
Printed in the USA
LVHW091247140221
679288LV00027B/293